MW01445390

SPANISH
MADE EASY

Omar Allibhoy

SIMPLE, MODERN
RECIPES FOR EVERY DAY

cover illustration by Jordan Amy Lee
photography by Martin Poole

Quadrille

Para Oscar, gracias por
enseñarme tanto. Te quiero

To my son Oscar, thanks for
teaching me so much. I love you

4	Introduction
6	My Spanish pantry
10	NIBBLES
34	MEAT & GAME
56	FISH & SEAFOOD
80	EGGS & POULTRY
96	VEGETABLES
114	SALADS
132	SOUPS, PULSES & STEWS
150	PAELLA & RICE
166	DESSERTS & SWEET TREATS
184	Index
190	Acknowledgements

INTRODUCTION

In this book I want to introduce you to the home-cooked meals that are widely enjoyed in my country, Spain, the food I grew up eating and that I cook every day at home for my family, the dinners that made our gastronomy so famous. My philosophy in the kitchen has always been the same: cook without fuss and eat like a king – quite simply. Eating great food is a luxury we all have the right to, so make the most of it.

I have a passion for Spanish food and tapas which I love to share – so much so that it has become my mission in life. I have felt this way ever since I left my beloved Madrid over a decade ago and I was exposed to other cuisines.

As a chef I had the pleasure and honour in my early years of training with and learning from some of the most talented chefs such as Ferran Adrià and Gordon Ramsay… As a diner I have travelled and eaten across dozens of countries, visited their restaurants, learned how they cook – but more importantly experienced how locals eat daily in their own homes with their loved ones.

It was on these travels that I began to realize how incredible, generous and tasty the food I grew up with was compared to the food I was discovering all over the world. Don't get me wrong: I love all food, but the dishes one grows up with leave an indelible mark on your heart, from the flavours, aromas and memories around them, to – in my case – the quick and easy dinners my mum used to rustle up in minutes, and the bigger family feasts where great conversation and laughter were vital ingredients around the table. Invariably, the most vivid memories of my life have centred around food with my family and friends.

Spain has a huge influx of tourists. I know I am a bit biased, but its popularity isn't surprising to me, as it's a sunny country blessed with beautiful and varied geography and landscapes, historically fascinating cities, stunning gastronomy and generally very funny and outgoing people with the greatest lifestyles. However, essentially what makes us all happy is not a location, the way the streets look or the weather, but actually the culture and lifestyle that we live and enjoy.

Working abroad for so long and running my own Spanish restaurants have given me the opportunity to appreciate the kinship so many people feel for my country when they first visit, which then turns into love when they come for the second time. This is the type of response that makes me feel very proud of my people and lucky about where I grew up.

I have experienced first-hand how much everyone loves our food and tapas, no matter where they themselves come from; it's the first thing they talk about when you ask them about Spain. I have concluded that food is one of the most important things in making a culture what it is because of how much pleasure we get from it and what it means to all of us.

I hope all this articulates why I am so passionate about Spanish food and why I have the urge to share it with you. My aim is to convince you to add some of my favourite dishes to your weekly repertoire.

Inside these pages you will find the best recipes I have to offer, for all sorts of occasions including quick midweek suppers, weekend lunches, full-on evening gatherings and, of course, some tapas. They have all been translated from my Spanish kitchen where most of the recipes are unwritten; they are just passed on verbally from generation to generation. They are authentic and simple – but some have necessitated a few phone calls to my mum and aunty, I must confess!

Food changes a lot through every season and every province across Spain to suit the local climate and produce. This is part of the beauty of the country – with such a wealth of variety, it feels like our gastronomy has infinite potential. The following recipes hail from every corner, from the hot Andalucía to the cooler Galicia, passing through historic Castilla and all the Mediterranean coast. I hope you'll find it a journey of discovery through the best-tasting and most authentic dishes.

I have tried to describe the recipes vividly and portray them as simply as I could so that no method, technique or ingredient sounds alien to anyone. You will find some shortcuts of the kind that I often employ at home, because unfortunately time is of the essence at Casa Allibhoy, too!

Buen provecho,

Omar

MY SPANISH PANTRY

Spanish cooking relies heavily on the quality and freshness of our ingredients. We are lucky to have an immense variety of diverse produce due to the physical geography of our land (mountains, woodlands, deserts...) and seas (Mediterranean, Atlantic), together with the very distinct climates we enjoy in our peninsula and islands. The mixture of cultures which have settled in Spain (the original Iberians, Phoenicians, Romans, Moors...) and even Spain's expeditions into the Americas, which brought so many vegetables which are staples in the Mediterranean diet today, have all brought new styles of cooking and recipes. Our way of eating is anarchic, in a way – at least mine, I must confess. That is why I love to have ingredients in my pantry which will serve me well at any time. Let me share with you the fundamental tools and foods I personally can't live without and which I would recommend you to keep in your cupboards. Don't worry if you can't get them all: everything in life is replaceable, other than our own will in the kitchen to make things work.

EQUIPMENT

Paella Pan (La Paella)
The paella pan, or 'la paella,' is the heart of Spain's most iconic dish. The pan's unique design allows rice to cook in a thin layer, creating the coveted socarrat (crispy bottom layer) that defines an authentic paella. Traditional pans can span over a meter in diameter for feeding entire villages, but at home you typically only need a 40cm (16in) version for family meals. This wide, shallow carbon steel pan with its distinctive flat bottom and slightly sloped sides isn't just for cooking Spanish rice dishes: at home I use it to cook pizzas, large tarte tatins or as the widest frying pan in my kitchen, for endless possibilities.

Clay Pots (Cazuelas)
These rustic earthenware vessels are the secret behind many of Spain's most beloved slow-cooked dishes. Traditional cazuelas are made from red clay, which retains heat beautifully and infuses food with a subtle earthy flavour that's impossible to replicate in metal cookware. From bubbling garlic prawns to hearty stews, these pots transform simple ingredients into dishes of remarkable depth. While they require some initial care (soaking before first use and gentle heating), their durability and versatility make them indispensable in any Spanish kitchen.

Pressure Cooker (Olla a Presión)

The pressure cooker holds a special place in modern Spanish home cooking, where it bridges traditional slow-cooking methods with contemporary time constraints. This essential tool reduces cooking times by up to 70% while maintaining the integrity of flavours in classic dishes like Potaje Montañés (see page 147).

INGREDIENTS

Paprika (Pimentón)

Pimentón is the soul of many Spanish dishes, coming in three distinct varieties: sweet (dulce), bittersweet (agridulce) and hot (picante). The most prized variety comes from La Vera, where peppers are slowly smoke-dried over oak, creating an intensely aromatic spice with an unmistakable smoky character. This deep red powder is essential for producing our chorizo and in dishes like Patatas Bravas (see page 26), as well as paellas, soups and stews.

Saffron (Azafrán)

Known as 'red gold,' Spanish saffron is the world's most expensive spice and a defining ingredient in Spanish cuisine. The finest comes from La Mancha, where crocus flowers are harvested by hand at dawn. Just a few threads of this precious spice – three to four per person – impart a distinctive orange colour and unique flavour to dishes like paella (see the chapter starting on page 150) and fish stews (such as on page 148). While expensive, its potency means a little goes a long way. Always pound with a pestle and mortar to extract maximum flavour from your precious threads.

Nuts (Frutos Secos)

Almonds, pine nuts, and hazelnuts are fundamental to Spanish cuisine, playing crucial roles in both sweet and savoury dishes. Almonds from Spain's Mediterranean coast are prized for their sweet, delicate flavour and are essential in treats like Turrón (see page 180) and sauces like Picada (see page 141). Pine nuts add richness to spinach dishes and traditional meat recipes, while hazelnuts feature prominently in Catalan cooking.

Sherry Wine and Vinegar (Vino de Jerez y Vinagre de Jerez)

Sherry and its vinegar, both from the sun-baked region of Jerez, are indispensable in Spanish cooking. Sherry ranges from bone-dry Fino (used on page 98) to rich Pedro Ximénez (used on page 171), each adding their own distinct character. The vinegar offers a complexity unmatched by regular wine vinegars. Its smooth, intense flavour transforms simple dishes like Gazpacho (see page 137) and aliños – dressings – such as on page 122.

Chorizo

Spain's most famous sausage is a masterpiece of spicing and curing. It is made from coarsely ground pork and distinctively marinated in pimentón (see page 7), which gives it both its characteristic taste and deep red color. Chorizo comes in two forms: fresh, raw sausages for cooking or cured versions for slicing or simmering for hours in a stew. Its intense, smoky paprika flavour makes it a powerful ingredient.

Spanish Ham (Jamón)

Spain's gastronomic treasure comes in two distinguished varieties, each representing different levels of ham-making artistry. The most prestigious is jamón ibérico, made from iberico breed pigs that roam freely in the dehesa woodlands, feeding partly on acorns (bellotas). This diet, combined with a curing process that can last over four years, creates a ham of unparalleled complexity – nutty, sweet and rich, with fat that literally melts at room temperature. Its more accessible cousin, jamón serrano (see photo on page 30), is made from white pigs and cured in similar conditions but for 12–24 months. The flavour is cleaner and less intense, yet still complex, which makes it perfect for everyday enjoyment. While ibérico, especially the covered ibérico de bellota, is the pinnacle of Spanish ham-making, Serrano is the backbone of our daily cuisine (featured on pages 18 and 136). It goes without saying that you can use any or both in all the recipes in this book.

Tomatoes (Tomates)

We love our tomatoes, and ours aren't just any tomatoes – they're sweeter, meatier, and full of flavour. Fresh tomatoes are used abundantly in summer dishes (see page 137), while high-quality canned tomatoes provide year-round consistency for sauces and stews. Always keep out of the fridge so they ripen properly.

Olive Oil (Aceite de Oliva)

The lifeblood of Spanish cuisine, extra virgin olive oil is used with almost religious devotion. Spain not only is the largest producer in the world, coping with about 50% of the worlds total production, it produces some of the world's finest oils, with varieties ranging from robust Picual to buttery Arbequina. This liquid gold is used not just for cooking but as a condiment in its own right. Spanish cooks often keep two types: a high-quality one for drizzling and finishing dishes, and a more economical version for cooking. Use generously.

Tuna and Tinned Fish (Conservas)
Spanish tinned seafood is a world away from ordinary canned fish. These conservas are a gourmet product, often better than fresh alternatives. From ventresca (tuna belly) to premium sardines and anchovies, these products are carefully prepared and packed in high-quality olive oil (never spring water). These aren't just convenience foods – they're delicacies in their own right.

Manchego Cheese
This iconic sheep's milk cheese from La Mancha is Spain's most famous dairy product. Aged from anywhere between 4 months to 2 years, Manchego develops from mild and creamy to sharp and crumbly. The genuine article, made only from Manchega sheep's milk, bears a distinctive herringbone pattern on its rind and offers complex flavours that can include notes of nuts, grass, and wax. Perfect on its own or with a piece of membrillo (quince jelly), it can elevate simple sandwiches (see page 28) or more elaborate tapas.

Olives (Aceitunas)
Spanish olives are far more than a pre-dinner snack. From tiny arbequinas to plump gordals, each variety offers unique flavours and textures. Many are cured with distinctive marinades featuring herbs, garlic, and peppers. These olives are essential for tapas but also add character to countless dishes (see page 64). The manzanilla variety, perhaps Spain's most famous, offers a perfect balance of flesh to pit and a clean, bright flavour that makes them ideal for both cooking and snacking.

Salt Cod (Bacalao Salado)
Bacalao has been a staple of Spanish cuisine for centuries. When properly soaked and prepared, this preserved fish transforms into tender, flaky flesh that's essential for dishes like bacalao al pil pil and Esgarraet Valenciano (see page 129). While it requires advance planning (soaking for 24–48 hours), the resulting versatility and unique flavour make it worth the effort. Quality bacalao should be pale white, with no yellow discoloration, and thick enough to maintain its structure when rehydrated.

Spanish Blood Sausage (Morcilla)
Morcilla, particularly the variety from Burgos, is a crucial ingredient in countless traditional dishes (see pages 52 and 165). Made with rice, onion and spices, it offers a rich, complex flavour, adding depth to stews and rice dishes. While it can be eaten cold, it's often grilled or fried until crispy on the outside but still creamy within. Regional varieties exist throughout Spain, all sharing a distinctive richness that makes them irreplaceable in Spanish cuisine.

de aperitivo
NIBBLES

SANGRÍA DE CAVA

SANGRIA MADE WITH CAVA

Cava, which is made in the same way as Champagne, has the edge over sparkling wines like prosecco, in my opinion. It has always been a celebration drink in Spain, but with prices being so affordable these days I thought I could make a sangria with it. The result is so refreshing, fruity and sharp.

Makes 2 litres (2 quarts)

1 orange
50g (3 tbsp) soft brown sugar
1 cinnamon stick
10 strawberries, quartered
1 pear, cored and roughly chopped
1 peach, roughly chopped
25ml (1½ tbsp) brandy
25ml (1½ tbsp) Cointreau
2 x 75cl bottles Spanish cava brut
fresh mint leaves (optional)

Refrigerate your glasses so that you can enjoy your drink as cold as possible.

Remove the zest of the orange in long strips. Squeeze the juice into a saucepan with the strips of zest, the sugar, cinnamon stick, the strawberries and the chopped pear and peach. Bring to the boil and cook for 1 minute. Pour into a jug or pitcher along with the brandy and Cointreau, stir with a wooden spoon and put in the fridge to chill until completely cold.

Stir the chilled mixture again and then pour 3 tablespoons into each glass. Top up with the fizzy cava, serve with a mint leaf, if you like, and enjoy it while it lasts.

BUÑUELOS DE BACALAO
SALT COD FRITTERS

Traditional buñuelos used to be sweet and were commonly sold in bakeries around Easter. With time, more developed recipes have arisen to bring us buñuelos made with savoury ingredients, such as cod (bacalao), cheese or even chard. These salt cod and cheese (see recipe overleaf) versions – both pictured here – are totally different; I urge you to try them both as they are seriously good.

Serves 8

125g (4½oz) boneless and skinless dried salt cod (bacalao) (you can use just fresh cod if you prefer, but you will lose a lot of the intensity of flavour)

2 potatoes (about 650g/1½lb)

200g (7oz) fresh cod

2 tbsp finely chopped chives

1 garlic clove, crushed

1 whole egg

1 tbsp plain (all-purpose) flour, if needed

sunflower oil, for deep-frying

Alioli (see page 27) or Romesco Sauce (see page 92), to serve

First, to rehydrate the salt cod, put it in a container and pour in enough cold water to cover. Leave overnight and change the water at least twice to extract as much salt as possible from the cod.

When you are ready to start cooking, peel and cut the potatoes into slices 1cm (½in) thick. Boil in unsalted water over a medium heat for about 15 minutes, or until cooked through. Drain and allow to dry.

Finely chop both the rehydrated salt cod and the fresh cod, removing any bones you find. Mix with the chives and garlic by hand or using a blender or food processor. Add the egg and boiled potatoes and mash together. Set aside for at least 10 minutes while you heat the oil. Depending on the potato and the size of your egg, the mixture could be a bit loose. If so, add the flour and the consistency should be better.

Pour enough oil into a deep pan to cover the base by about 3cm (1¼in). Heat until a cube of day-old bread dropped into the oil turns golden in about 30 seconds. Alternatively, heat a deep fryer to 180°C (360°F).

Drop tablespoonfuls of the mixture into the hot oil and fry until they float and turn light golden, up to 2 minutes. Remove from the oil with a slotted spoon and drain on paper towels while you finish the fritters. Serve with alioli or romesco sauce.

Pictured left, top.

BUÑUELOS DE QUESO
CHEESE FRITTERS

Serves 4 as a tapa

45g (3½ tbsp) butter

2g (½ tsp) table salt

75g (9 tbsp) plain (all-purpose) flour

1 egg, beaten

50g (½ cup) grated Manchego or Cheddar cheese

1 garlic clove, finely chopped

1 spring onion (scallion), thinly sliced

vegetable oil, for deep-frying

Alioli (see page 27) or Romesco Sauce (see page 92), to serve

Place 7 tablespoons of water, the butter and salt in a pan and bring to the boil. Add the flour, remove from the heat and mix with a wooden spoon for about 30 seconds until it is well combined and the mixture has become a ball that pulls away from the sides of the pan. Take off the heat.

Add the egg and stir it into the dough until fully incorporated. The mixture should have the consistency of thick yogurt at this point. Add the grated cheese, garlic and spring onion and mix until well combined.

Pour enough oil into a deep pan to cover the base by about 3cm (1¼in). Heat until a cube of day-old bread dropped into the oil turns golden in about 30 seconds. Alternatively, heat a deep fryer to 180°C (360°F).

Use a couple of spoons to start dropping in knobs of dough about the size of a walnut. The dough should start frying and puff up immediately and after a few seconds they will turn over by themselves. Leave them in the oil until they turn golden brown, about 2 minutes, then scoop out with a slotted spoon and drain on kitchen paper. Cook in batches so that the oil doesn't cool down too much. Your buñuelos should have a delicate crispness on the outside and be pretty much all air on the inside. Serve with alioli or romesco sauce.

Pictured on page 14, bottom.

EMPANADILLAS DE QUESO Y ESPINACA

PASTRY PARCELS FILLED WITH SPINACH, RAISINS AND GOAT CHEESE

I grew up eating these (like every Spanish kid, really) but traditionally they tend to be filled with tuna, red (bell) peppers and tomato. This vegetarian version is so tasty and so popular in my restaurants.

Serves 8 as a tapa

For the dough
5 tbsp olive oil
175g (1⅓ cups) plain (all-purpose) flour, plus extra to dust
a pinch of salt
1 egg, beaten

For the filling
5 tbsp olive oil
1 onion, thinly sliced
2 garlic cloves, finely chopped
3 tbsp raisins
200g (scant 4 cups) baby spinach (or use frozen)
50g (2oz) goat cheese
a pinch of salt
a pinch of white pepper
2 tbsp double (heavy) cream

To make the dough, pour the oil and 5 tablespoons of water into a saucepan over a high heat and bring to the boil. Take off the heat and add the flour and salt, stirring vigorously for about 1 minute, or until fully mixed. Allow to cool a little, then turn out and knead for 1 minute. Wrap in plastic wrap and refrigerate for 30 minutes.

Roll out the chilled pastry on a lightly floured surface to about 3mm (⅛in) thick and cut out as many circles as you can using a saucer as a template. Re-roll the scraps to make more circles. Set aside.

Pour the olive oil for the filling into a large frying pan and gently fry the onion over a medium heat for a good 20 minutes, or until golden. Add the garlic and raisins and fry with the onion for a further 5 minutes. Add the spinach, crumble in the goat cheese and season with the salt and pepper. Let it all wilt and melt for a couple of minutes and then add the cream. Don't leave it over the heat for longer than 2 minutes. Allow to cool, then refrigerate for at least 30 minutes so that it becomes easier to handle.

Preheat the oven to 200°C/180°C fan/400°F/gas mark 6.

Spread the pastry discs over the worktop and add a tablespoon of the filling to each one. Brush all around the edges with the beaten egg, then fold each one over to make semi-circles. Use a fork to press the edges together to seal. Brush each empanadilla with more egg and bake for 10 minutes, or until golden and crispy.

Easy tip
These can also be shallow-fried in oil over a medium heat for 2 minutes on each side.

CHAMPIÑONES GRATINADOS

MUSHROOM GRATIN WITH HAM MAYONNAISE

Serves 4 as a tapa

4 portobello mushrooms, stalks trimmed

2 sprigs fresh thyme, leaves separated

olive oil

the green part of 1 spring onion (scallion), finely chopped

sea salt and freshly ground black pepper

For the ham mayonnaise

1 egg yolk

1 garlic clove

a pinch of salt

1 tbsp lemon juice or vinegar

3 slices Serrano ham, roughly chopped

150ml (scant ⅔ cup) mild olive oil

This simple recipe carries an explosion of flavour. It makes a great starter (appetizer) when you are entertaining friends or family, as you can leave it hot in the oven until you need it. I use portobello mushrooms but you can use any flat mushroom, or even large oyster types.

Place the mushrooms on a roasting tray and sprinkle with sea salt, a bit of black pepper, the fresh thyme leaves and a drizzle of olive oil. Place in a cold oven and set the temperature to 180°C/160°C fan/350°F/gas mark 4. Bake for 15 minutes.

Meanwhile, for the ham mayonnaise, blend the egg yolk, garlic clove, salt, lemon juice and ham in a food processor and then start to add the oil in a steady stream until you have a mayonnaise.

Remove the tray from the oven and sprinkle the mushrooms with the chopped spring onion. Top with a dollop of the ham mayonnaise and return to the oven for a good 5 minutes, or until the top has nicely browned.

TOSTA DE HIGOS CON JAMÓN

PAN-FRIED FIGS, SERRANO HAM, CREAM CHEESE AND WALNUTS ON TOAST

Tapas are much easier to make at home than people think, and these days you can find most Spanish ingredients in your local supermarket so there is no excuse. Figs are at their peak in early autumn; make sure you buy soft and sweet ones.

Serves 4 as a tapa

100g (½ cup) cream cheese
50g (½ cup) walnut halves
4 slices rustic bread, toasted
8 figs
extra virgin olive oil
1 tbsp brown sugar
a splash of sherry vinegar
a pinch of rock or sea salt
8 thin slices Serrano ham

Mix the cream cheese with three-quarters of the walnuts, crumbling them between your hands and beating them into the cheese with a fork. Spread generously over the bread.

Open your figs by cutting a cross at the pointed end and opening them out like a flower with your fingers.

Drizzle some olive oil into a pan over a medium heat and add the brown sugar. Add the figs and fry the bases only, without turning them; we only want to cook the bottoms of the figs. Watch that the caramel that forms in the pan doesn't burn. Add the sherry vinegar and turn off the heat.

Place your hot figs over the toasts and drizzle with the hot vinaigrette from the pan. Top with a good drizzle of extra virgin olive oil, a pinch of salt and the slices of Serrano ham. Sprinkle with the remaining walnuts.

Easy swap
Try this recipe with melon instead of figs – it will be equally great.

ANCHOAS CON VINAGRE Y PIMENTÓN

SALTED ANCHOVIES WITH PAPRIKA AND VINEGAR

Serves 3 as an apertivo

1 x 50g (2oz) tin (can) salted anchovies (or sardines) in oil

3 tbsp extra virgin olive oil

a pinch of sweet pimentón (sweet smoked paprika)

1 tbsp sherry vinegar

1 bag of plain crisps (potato chips), to serve

You probably wouldn't imagine that a salted anchovy could actually be marinated. You will be very surprised by how much it can change with just this small touch, and for the better!

Drain the oil from the anchovies.

Mix together the extra virgin olive oil with the pimentón and vinegar and pour over the anchovies. Let them marinate for 5 minutes and enjoy each anchovy on top of a crisp, as is a tradition in tapas bars across Spain.

BANDERILLAS

SKEWERED PICKLES

Pickled banderillas – customized skewers with your favourite pickles – are another ubiquitous tapa in bars around Spain. We love all pickles; in our supermarkets you will find a wide range of brined vegetables, from garlic to artichokes, and fish, from mussels to anchovies. The vinegar flavour tastes exciting in your mouth and it is the perfect match for a beer or two, as an aperitivo. In Spain you can find banderillas ready made, but we prefer to make them ourselves and choose the ingredients we fancy.

Makes as many as you like!

white or salted anchovies
green Spanish queen olives
green chilli peppers in brine (preferably hot Spanish green)
pickled silver (pearl or baby) onions
gherkins
extra virgin olive oil

18cm (7in) wooden skewers or strong cocktail sticks (toothpicks)

Roll an anchovy around an olive and poke a skewer through the middle, getting both sides of the fish and making sure they are well stacked. Next, introduce a chilli pepper. Because they are normally quite long, I recommend you cut it in half or fold it over. Follow this with a baby onion and lastly, introduce the gherkin. This ingredient should not be missing in any combination; it is the main pickle of the banderilla. Prick the gherkin horizontally. Of course, you can change the order of the ingredients, as you like.

Repeat to make all the skewers you require. Pour over a drizzle of extra virgin olive oil and serve.

PATATAS BRAVAS

FRIED POTATOES WITH SPICY TOMATO SAUCE

I was born in Madrid, hence I love my patatas bravas, a real staple tapa where I come from. You will find endless recipes and styles for the same dish; in some places they are served with alioli mixed with the spicy sauce. It is definitely one of the more simple and typical tapas of our gastronomy, and the most popular in all tapas bars.

Serves 4 as a tapa

- 2–3 large Maris Piper or other floury potatoes, peeled
- mild olive or sunflower oil, for deep-frying
- or
- olive oil, a few rosemary sprigs, a few crushed garlic cloves, salt and freshly ground black pepper, for roasting
- Alioli, to serve (see opposite)

For the sauce

- 50ml (3 tbsp) extra virgin olive oil
- 1 garlic clove, thinly sliced
- ½ onion, thinly sliced
- 2 dried cayenne chilli peppers (this is enough, I swear)
- ½ bay leaf
- 1 tbsp white vinegar
- a pinch of dried oregano
- a pinch of ground cumin
- 1 tsp sweet paprika
- 250ml (generous 1 cup) tomato passata (or strained or milled tinned tomatoes)

Start by cooking the sauce. In a small saucepan set over a medium heat, pour in the olive oil and add the onion, garlic, cayenne and bay leaf. Cook for about 10 minutes until soft. Add the vinegar, oregano, cumin and paprika, let the mixture boil for 30 seconds and then add the passata. Cook for a further 15 minutes. Set aside to cool a little, then blend until silky-smooth.

For the potatoes, it could be as simple as cutting them into wedges. Now, I like my bravas cut in irregular chunks, let's say about 2.5cm (1in) big. However you choose to cut them, put them into a pan of cold water, bring them to the boil and then simmer for about 15 minutes, or until soft. Drain and leave to dry completely.

Pour enough oil into a deep pan to fill it to about one-third full. Heat until a cube of day-old bread dropped into the oil turns golden in about 30 seconds. Alternatively, heat a deep fryer to 180°C (360°F). Cook half the potatoes for about 5 minutes to create the crunchy outer crust. Repeat with the rest of the potatoes. Alternatively, roast the potatoes for 30 minutes at 200°C/180°C fan/400°F/gas mark 6, with a bit of olive oil, a few rosemary sprigs, a few crushed garlic cloves, salt and pepper. The result is also very good.

Serve the cooked potatoes with the warm sauce poured over the top. You could also add a spoonful of Alioli (see opposite). A refreshing cold beer is my suggestion to match this tapa and to cope with the hot sauce!

ALIOLI

GARLIC MAYONNAISE

Alioli is such a versatile sauce and it combines well with so many dishes. It can be fine-tuned to incorporate a distinctive flavour and accompany specific types of food, for example saffron, lime, pimentón – you name it.

Makes about 250g (1 cup), or serves 8

1 egg
2 garlic cloves
1 tbsp lemon juice
½ tsp salt
100ml (scant ½ cup) vegetable oil
100ml (scant ½ cup) extra virgin olive oil

Put the egg, garlic, lemon juice, salt and a drizzle of either oil in a small jug. Using a stick blender, blitz all the ingredients together. With the blender still going, very slowly trickle in the remaining oils until they have all been added and the alioli has completely emulsified.

If you are unlucky enough that your alioli splits, just start again with a bit of water in the jug before pouring the split mixture into it and blitzing it again.

Easy variations
For a plain mayonnaise, leave out the garlic, reduce the lemon juice to ½ tbsp and use 200ml (scant 1 cup) extra virgin oil instead of a combination. Take a glass jar wide enough to fit a hand blender and pour all the ingredients into it. Let them sit for 1 minute. Now put the hand blender in the bottom of the jar and blend – the egg and lemon juice will emulsify first. Slowly tilt and lift the hand blender up through the ingredients for about 30 seconds – the oil will emulsify at this stage and your mayonnaise will not split. This is exactly how mayonnaise is made in Spain!

Alioli can be turned into something completely different and become a key ingredient in its own right if blended with some more substantial extras. This is a popular technique in Spain when making canapés at home, or at least in my family, where we add grated Manchego cheese in generous amounts and spread it on toast. Another good variation is to add some finely chopped mussels preserved in escabeche or cockles in brine, then fill vols-au-vent or tartlets with the alioli and sprinkle some snipped chives on top.

BOCADILLOS VARIADOS
ASSORTED SANDWICHES

These are Spanish takes on regular sandwiches, perfect for any occasion: a picnic, to bring to work, to a football match, for school… Actually, when I was a kid we had a healthy competition at school to see who brought in the best bocadillo every day for the break.

Sandwiches pictured overleaf.

ALMUSSAFES
CHORIZO PÂTÉ AND CHEESE SANDWICH

Makes 1
a drizzle of olive oil
a small knob of butter
½ small onion, finely chopped
1 small rustic ciabatta bread, sliced in half
Sobrasada de Mallorca (see page 76) or 5 chorizo slices
1 tsp honey
30g (1oz) Manchego, thinly sliced

Heat the oil and butter in a pan over a medium heat and add the onion. Cook for about 10 minutes, or until soft and golden. Set aside. Toast the bread halves in the same pan. Spread one of the halves with the sobrasada, or lay the chorizo slices over the top, and drizzle with the honey. Top with the caramelized onion and cheese. Close the sandwich and be happy.

PEPITO DE TERNERA
BEEF SANDWICH

Makes 1
a small knob of butter
1 small rustic ciabatta bread, sliced in half
2 thin beef steaks, preferably sirloin (strip steak) or bavette (flap steak)
salt and freshly ground black pepper
chips (fries) to serve, optional

Melt the butter in a pan over a medium heat and fry the bread. Set aside. Put the steak in the same pan over a high heat, season with salt and pepper and cook to your liking. Assemble the sandwich and enjoy freshly made with some chips on the side, if you like.

Note
This sandwich doesn't travel well!

MEDIA LUNA DE ATÚN Y ALIOLI

TUNA AND ALIOLI BRIOCHE SANDWICH WITH PIQUILLO PEPPERS

Makes 1

1 brioche roll or 'pain au lait' (milk loaf), sliced in half

1 tbsp tinned tuna in oil, drained

2 tbsp Alioli or Mayonnaise (see both on page 27)

2 cooked white asparagus from a tin/jar, halved

1 piquillo pepper, sliced in half lengthways

a sprinkling of shredded lettuce

Toast the roll halves over a hot pan or under a grill (broiler). Mix the tuna with the alioli or mayonnaise and spread it over one half of the brioche. Top with the asparagus, piquillo pepper and lettuce. Close the roll and serve.

BOCADILLO DE CALAMARES

DEEP-FRIED SQUID SANDWICH

Makes 1

vegetable oil, for deep-frying

100g (3½oz) frozen squid tubes, thinly sliced into rings or strips

2 tbsp plain (all-purpose) flour

1 mini baguette, sliced in half

2 tbsp Mayonnaise (see page 27)

salt

This is a truly Madrileño speciality. It sounds crazy but when I go to Madrid to visit the family, I can't leave without having one of these.

Pour enough oil into a deep pan to cover the base by about 3cm (1¼in). Heat until a cube of day-old bread dropped into the oil turns golden in about 30 seconds. Alternatively, heat a deep fryer to 180°C (360°F).

Lightly coat the squid in the flour and drop loosely into the hot oil. Fry for about 90 seconds, or until crispy. Drain and season with salt. Spread one half of the baguette with a bit of mayonnaise before stuffing the squid into it. Enjoy hot.

Note
This sandwich doesn't travel well!

COCA DE REQUENA

MEAT FOCACCIA

Serves 6

For the dough
7g (scant 1 tsp) dried yeast
230ml (1 cup) warm water
300g (2 cups + 2 tbsp) strong white bread flour, plus extra to dust
50ml (2 tbsp) olive oil
3g (heaped ½ tsp) salt

For the toppings
1 cooking chorizo (fresh uncooked) sausage, chopped
2 pork sausages, chopped
3 slices streaky bacon or pancetta, cut in half
2 slices black pudding (blood sausage), chopped, optional

Across Spain we combine a variety of leavened breads, rolls and flatbreads with other ingredients. This version reminds me of a British 'toad in the hole', but made with a focaccia-like bread instead of batter. All the rendered fats from the meats are absorbed into the bread, resulting in a very indulgent experience.

First make the dough. In a large bowl, mix together the yeast and warm water and stir until dissolved. Mix the flour with the oil and salt and tip this into the bowl. Knead for at least 6–8 minutes, until you can bring the dough together with your hands. Cover with a cloth and allow to rest at room temperature for 1 hour.

Preheat the oven to 200°C/180°C fan/400°F/gas mark 6.

Dust a work surface with flour and roll out the dough to an oval shape about 2cm (¾in) thick and place it on a baking sheet. Top with the chorizo, sausages, bacon and black pudding, if using, and press them gently into the dough.

Bake for about 16 minutes, or until the bread has risen and looks crisp and golden and the toppings have released their fats. Tear into pieces at the table.

carnes y caza
MEAT & GAME

CORDERO AL CHILINDRÓN

SLOW-COOKED LAMB AND PEPPER STEW

Serves 4

1kg (2lb 3oz) diced lamb

a pinch of ground cumin

100g (¾ cup) plain (all-purpose) flour

75ml (5 tbsp) olive oil

2 large carrots, cut into thin strips

1 large onion, cut into thin strips

3 garlic cloves, thinly sliced

1 red (bell) pepper, cut into thin strips

½ green (bell) pepper, cut into thin strips

a few bay leaves

1 sprig fresh thyme, plus extra to garnish

4 tomatoes, peeled and chopped

a pinch of sugar

1 tsp sweet pimentón (sweet smoked paprika)

200ml (scant 1 cup) white wine

salt and freshly ground black pepper

crusty bread or fried diced potatoes, to serve

This dish is commonly found in northern Spain and was always cooked in the spring with the new lamb season. It's one of those ugly brown but very tasty slow-cooked stews Spain is famous for. We also use other meats for this dish, such as goat or chicken.

Season the lamb with salt, pepper and just a little pinch of ground cumin, then coat with the flour. Heat the olive oil in a deep, heavy-based pan (with a lid) over a high heat and toss the coated lamb in the pan for about 5 minutes to seal the edges. Remove the lamb, leaving the oil in the pan, and set it aside to rest.

Add the carrots, onion, garlic and peppers to the pan along with the bay leaves and thyme and reduce the heat to medium. Cook for 10 minutes and then add the chopped tomatoes with the sugar and cook for a further 5 minutes, until the ingredients are combined to make a tomato paste, or sofrito.

Add the lamb back to the pan with the sweet pimentón, white wine and 1 litre (4⅓ cups) water and cook, covered, over a low heat for a couple of hours, or until the meat is tender, adding more water if necessary. The result should be a rich, dense and silky sauce. Garnish with fresh thyme and serve with crusty bread or fried diced potatoes, if you like.

CHULETITAS DE CORDERO MARINADAS
MOORISH MARINATED LAMB CUTLETS

Serves 4 as a main or 8 as a tapa

12 lamb cutlets (chops)

2 garlic cloves, finely chopped

10 sprigs fresh thyme, leaves removed, plus extra to serve

200ml (scant 1 cup) olive oil

1 tbsp honey

2 tsp ground cumin

2 tsp dried oregano

1 tsp sweet or hot pimentón (sweet or hot smoked paprika)

a pinch of salt

freshly ground black pepper

Frisée lettuce, Pomegranate and Olive Salad (see page 130), to serve, optional

These Moorish spiced lamb cutlets are to die for. You can actually use any meat to prepare this dish, such as pork chops or chicken drumsticks. The key is in the marinade. If you are planning a BBQ, don't overlook this recipe.

Place all the ingredients except the meat in a large mixing bowl. Whisk until well combined, then add the lamb cutlets, making sure they are well coated. Marinate for at least 1 hour or up to 2 days, covered, in the fridge.

Remove any excess marinade from the meat and cook on a very hot dry griddle or frying pan for 2 minutes on each side if you like your meat pink, or 4 minutes if you like it well done. Take care not to burn the outsides. You could also cook them over charcoal or under the grill (broiler) for 10 minutes. Sprinkle with the thyme leaves and some sea salt flakes before serving, if you like.

If you're serving as a main meal this works really well alongside the frisée lettuce, pomegranate and olive salad.

MACARRONES CON TOMATE Y CHORIZO

PENNE PASTA WITH CHORIZO AND TOMATO SAUCE

Serves 4

1 small onion, chopped
2 garlic cloves, sliced
1 chorizo sausage, diced
3½ tbsp olive oil
2 x 400g (14oz) tins chopped tomatoes
1 tsp dried oregano
1 tbsp sugar
350g (12oz) penne pasta
salt, optional
a sprinkling of grated Parmesan, to serve

This dish is so popular back home, to the extent that it was a school meal when I was a kid. The chorizo sausage makes a wonderful and rich tomato sauce that, combined with the penne pasta and cheese, turns this into a great lunch or dinner.

Place the onion, garlic, chorizo and olive oil in a large pan over a medium heat. Cook for about 5 minutes, stirring, until the onion is soft and the chorizo has released its juices. Add the chopped tomatoes, oregano and sugar and cook until the sauce is rich and has reduced by at least two-thirds. Taste and add salt if needed.

In a separate large pan, bring 2 litres (2 quarts) water to the boil, then add the pasta. Cook following the manufacturer's instructions, but drain 2 minutes before the time is over, then add the pasta to the tomato sauce with 100ml (scant ½ cup) of the cooking water. Give it a good stir over a high heat to mix all the ingredients thoroughly. Serve with a sprinkling of grated Parmesan cheese.

TORREZNOS CON MOJO DULCE

SLOW-COOKED PORK BELLY WITH A SWEET, SPICY AND SOUR SAUCE

Serves 4

1kg (2lb 3oz) pork belly

1 tbsp rock salt

250ml (generous 1 cup) white wine or beer

600g (1lb 5oz) new potatoes

For the mojo dulce sauce

6 dried cayenne or bird's eye chilli peppers, finely chopped

1 tsp ground cumin

1 tsp sweet pimentón (sweet smoked paprika)

1 tsp black pepper powder

1 tsp ground cinnamon

1 tsp dried oregano

1 tsp salt

75ml (⅓ cup) sherry vinegar

3½ tbsp extra virgin olive oil

100g (scant ½ cup) sugar

Who doesn't like slow-cooked, soft pork belly? And if, to something this scrumptious, you add the mojo dulce sauce that hundreds of customers I have catered for have asked me to bottle and sell, then I think we have a winner.

Preheat the oven to 160°C/140°C fan/325°F/gas mark 3.

Score the skin of the pork belly using the tip of a sharp knife to make even incisions running the length of the meat. Place in a glass or ceramic roasting dish, skin-side up, rub with the rock salt and pour the wine or beer around the meat. Slow-cook for 4 hours. Add the new potatoes around the meat in the dish 1½ hours before the end of the cooking time.

To make the mojo dulce sauce, first measure all the spices, the oregano and the salt into a small bowl. Measure out the sherry vinegar, olive oil and 200ml (scant 1 cup) water.

Pour another 3½ tablespoons of water into a small saucepan over a medium heat and add the sugar. Allow the sugar to melt, without stirring, to make a syrup. When the syrup turns to amber, tip in all the dried spices and give them a good stir for about 10 seconds. The caramel will toast the spices very quickly so don't leave them any longer. Pour the vinegar, oil and water mixture straight into the pan and keep stirring so that the caramel dissolves. Simmer over a low heat for 10 minutes and then take a hand blender, while the pan is still over the heat, and blitz for 1 minute to emulsify the sauce. Keep the blender away from the heat source.

Serve your pork belly with the roasted new potatoes and pour the thick mojo dulce over the top.

Easy tip

If you have any leftovers, shred the pork belly, mix it with a bit of the sauce, put some cheese over it and make a really good crusty-bread sandwich.

Recipe pictured overleaf.

CHORIZO AL VINO

CHORIZO COOKED IN WINE

Add chorizo to any dish and it will be transformed into something really tasty. In this case chorizo is the main event, so prepare yourself for an explosion of flavour. All you need is just three ingredients and a pan and you'll have a great tapa to surprise your guests with.

Serves 6 as a tapa

4 cooking chorizo (fresh uncooked) sausages
175ml (scant ¾ cup) white wine
1 tsp soft brown sugar
1 bay leaf
bread, to serve

Place the whole sausages in a pan together with the wine, sugar and bay leaf. Cook over a high heat for about 15 minutes. The wine should eventually reduce down to a rich syrup.

Remove the sausages from the sauce and cut them into thick slices. Serve as a tapa with some bread to dip in the sauce.

CACHOPO ASTURIANO

SPANISH CORDON BLEU

It may sound ridiculous, but this has been the most on-trend dish for the last few years back in Spain. So, if you travel there, and not just in Asturias – I mean anywhere across the peninsula – order one. It is in essence a fried, breadcrumbed steak wrapped in ham and cheese. As messy as it sounds, believe me, it's worth the fuss!

Serves 4

4 tbsp plain (all-purpose) flour
100g (2 cups) breadcrumbs
2 eggs, beaten
4 rump (sirloin) steaks, fat removed
4 slices smoked ham
4 slices cheddar
4 slices Serrano ham
salt and freshly ground black pepper
olive oil, for frying

Spread out the flour on one plate, the breadcrumbs on another and tip the beaten eggs into a shallow bowl.

Use a meat tenderizer or rolling pin to flatten the steaks as thinly as possible without breaking them.

Take one of the flattened steaks and lay a slice of the smoked ham over one half. Lay a slice of cheddar on top and then a slice of the Serrano ham. Sprinkle with salt and freshly ground black pepper. Wrap the steak over the filling like you're closing a book. Repeat until all of the steaks are filled.

Take one steak and coat it first in flour, then egg and finally breadcrumbs. Repeat with the rest of the steaks.

Heat some oil in a wide frying pan set over a medium heat. When the oil is hot, add the steaks to the pan and fry for 2 minutes on each side until perfectly golden. Drain any excess oil and enjoy while hot.

Recipe pictured overleaf.

ALBÓNDIGAS A LA TRUFA
MEATBALLS IN BLACK TRUFFLE SAUCE

Serves 4

2 slices white bread (crusts removed), broken into pieces

140ml (scant ⅔ cup) whole milk

500g (2¼ cups) finely minced (ground) beef (or a mixture of meats, such as pork, chicken or turkey)

100g (½ cup) meat pâté

salt and freshly ground black pepper

plain (all-purpose) flour, for dusting

olive oil, for frying

crusty bread, to serve

For the black truffle sauce

25g (1½ tbsp) butter

a drizzle of olive oil

1 bunch spring onions (scallions), finely chopped

1 carrot, finely chopped

75g (1 heaped cup) button or oyster mushrooms, finely chopped

25g (3½ tbsp) plain (all-purpose) flour

4 tbsp white wine

500ml (2 cups) beef, chicken or vegetable stock

1 tsp salt

1 tsp finely chopped rosemary

100ml (scant ½ cup) double (heavy) cream

2 black truffles

Truffles are delicate in flavour and aroma. Spain is one of the biggest producers of black truffles in Europe, supplying top restaurants all over the world. You can get them in brine in supermarkets these days, which is handy.

Place the bread in a bowl and pour over the milk. Set aside to soak.

In a separate bowl, mix together the meat and the pâté. Add the soaked bread and season with salt and freshly ground black pepper. Mix until smooth and well combined. Form meatballs by rolling walnut-sized pieces of the mixture between your hands. They should be about 30g (1oz) each. Dust the meatballs in flour.

Heat some oil in a shallow pan over a medium-high heat and fry the meatballs just until they are golden. Do not overcook at this stage as we are going to finish them in the sauce. Set aside.

To make the sauce, heat the butter and olive oil in a pan over a medium-low heat and add the spring onions, carrot and mushrooms. Cook for about 10 minutes, stirring, until the onion is transparent. Reduce the temperature to low and add the flour to the pan, stirring with a wooden spoon to make a roux. Cook for about 4 minutes and then add the wine, continuing to stir until you get a paste and the alcohol has evaporated, then add the stock with the salt and rosemary. Keep stirring and cooking until the sauce thickens, then add the cream, stirring so that the mixture doesn't split or curdle. Add the meatballs to the sauce and cook for a further 5 minutes.

Grate the truffles into the sauce and serve immediately, with crusty bread, as the truffles lose their aroma quickly.

CONEJO EN SALMOREJO

RABBIT WITH A CANARY ISLANDS SAUCE

This dish is from our beloved Canary Islands. We call them the fortunate islands because the sun is always shining down there. This gently spicy, intensely flavoured salmorejo sauce is not to be confused with the thick tomato, bread and oil soup of the same name that's typical of Córdoba in southern Spain.

Serves 4

- 200ml (scant 1 cup) white wine
- a drizzle of extra virgin olive oil
- 1 tbsp dried oregano
- 4 garlic cloves, chopped, plus 6 whole, unpeeled
- 1 tbsp sweet pimentón (sweet smoked paprika)
- 1 small dried chilli pepper, chopped
- 1 whole rabbit, cut into 8 pieces
- 1 bay leaf
- 5 sprigs fresh thyme
- olive oil, for frying
- 400ml (1¾ cups) chicken stock
- rock or sea salt and freshly ground black pepper

In a bowl or food processor, blend together 2 tablespoons of the white wine, a drizzle of extra virgin olive oil, the oregano, chopped garlic, sweet pimentón and the chopped chilli. Rub this marinade over the pieces of rabbit, add the whole garlic cloves, bay leaf and thyme and refrigerate, covered, overnight if you have the time, otherwise never mind.

Heat a good drizzle of olive oil in a large frying pan over a high heat. Remove the excess marinade from the rabbit (keep it for later), sprinkle with salt and pan-fry the pieces for about 3 minutes on each side, or until browned. Season with salt and pepper.

Add the leftover marinade to the pan, including the bay leaf and thyme, and fry for a further 4 minutes. Add the remaining white wine and allow to reduce down completely before adding the chicken stock. Simmer all together for 10 minutes, shaking the pan now and then to form a rich, intense sauce.

MORCILLA DE BURGOS CON MANZANA

SPANISH BLACK PUDDING WITH CARAMELIZED APPLE

I have a weakness for black pudding (and offal in general). To me, it's a total delicacy, so good that I don't like to eat it too often otherwise it stops being special. I do the same with jamón ibérico. In this dish the apple and honey are the perfect match for the main event.

Serves 4 as a tapa

- 3 tbsp extra virgin olive oil
- 1 x large Morcilla de Burgos (Spanish rice black pudding made with rice)
- 1 cinnamon stick, broken
- 2 apples, any variety, cored and cut into wedges
- 1 tbsp pine nuts
- 1 tbsp honey
- a pinch of sea salt
- bread, to serve

Cut the black pudding into finger-width slices and set aside.

Heat the olive oil in a frying pan over a high heat and cook the black pudding slices for 2 minutes on each side so that the edges are crispy. Remove to a plate.

Reduce the heat to medium, then add the cinnamon stick and the apple wedges. Cook for at least 3 minutes on each side, adding the pine nuts to the pan for the last 3 minutes. Drizzle the honey into the pan and continue to cook until the apples are lightly caramelized. Season with a pinch of salt.

Add the morcilla back the pan and heat until warmed through, then serve together on a plate and enjoy with lots of good bread.

ESTOFADO DE CORZO CON SETAS

VENISON AND WILD MUSHROOM STEW WITH OLIVE MASH (MY FAMILY STYLE)

Serves 6

2kg (4½lb) shoulder of venison
1 x 75cl bottle Spanish red wine
olive oil, for frying
1 carrot, roughly chopped
1 celery stick, roughly chopped
1 onion, roughly chopped
2 tomatoes, chopped
2 bay leaves
1 sprig fresh thyme
1 sprig fresh rosemary
1 sprig fresh marjoram
5 black peppercorns
2 cloves
½ cinnamon stick
2½ tbsp brandy
500g (1lb 2oz) wild mushrooms
570ml (2½ cups) beef stock
salt

For the mashed potatoes

1kg (2lb 3oz) waxy potatoes
200g (¾ cup + 2 tbsp) butter
100ml (scant ½ cup) olive oil
100ml (scant ½ cup) double (heavy) cream
salt and freshly ground black pepper

In autumn and winter my uncles and cousins would go hunting in the mountains of Madrid, but not all of us liked hunting, so we used to pick mushrooms along the way. This was a dish that would be on the table a couple of days later, after we'd chopped up and marinated the animal.

Cut the venison into big chunks, pour over the red wine and leave to marinate in the fridge overnight.

The next day, drain the wine and reserve it for later. Heat some olive oil in a large deep heavy-based pan (with a lid) or roasting tray over a high heat and, working in batches, fry the venison pieces to seal them. Remove and set aside. If you plan to slow-cook the stew in the oven, preheat it to 160°C/140°C fan/325°F/gas mark 3.

Add a little more oil to the pan and add the carrot, celery and onion. Cook, stirring, for 20 minutes until caramelized and then add the tomatoes, herbs and spices. Return the meat to the pan and pour over the brandy and reserved wine. Cook until reduced by half.

Add the wild mushrooms and the beef stock and season with a little salt. Bring to the boil and then cover with the lid or with foil. Slow-cook the stew either over a low heat or in the oven for at least 3 hours, or until the meat falls apart and you have an unctuous and rich sauce. Leave the oven on.

To make the mashed potatoes, if you are cooking the venison on the hob, heat the oven to 160°C/140°C fan/325°F/gas mark 3 now. Peel, wash and cut the potatoes into even slices and place them in a large pan. Cover with cold water and bring to the boil over a high heat. Cook for about 15 minutes until soft, then drain and return to the same pan. Set over a low heat for 1 minute to dry. Add the butter, salt and pepper and start mashing using a potato masher or whisk. Add the olive oil and cream and mix. Tip onto a baking sheet and bake on the top shelf of the oven for 20 minutes so that it crisps up and lightly browns. Serve hot with the venison stew.

pescados y mariscos
FISH & SEAFOOD

MERLUZA A LA GALLEGA

GALICIAN-STYLE HAKE

A dish with soft, subtle flavours – nothing punchy – that is all good and healthy. Sometimes comfort is found in the most basic form of cooking. Call me crazy but I find this dish sublime.

Serves 4

2 medium onions, peeled and halved

1 tbsp salt, plus extra for seasoning

1 bay leaf

4 medium white potatoes, halved

4 hake steaks or fillets

100ml (scant ½ cup) olive oil

4 garlic cloves, sliced

1 tsp sweet pimentón (sweet smoked paprika)

freshly ground black pepper

Place a large deep pan over a high heat. Add 800ml (3½ cups) water, the salt, onions and bay leaf. Bring to the boil, add the potatoes and cook for about 13 minutes, or until the vegetables are half cooked.

Season the hake with salt and pepper and add it to the water with the potatoes, making sure they are completely covered by water and adding more if necessary. Cook for another 6 minutes and then remove from the heat. Carefully remove the delicate fish and potatoes from the pan, keeping the fish whole. Set aside 150ml (scant ⅔ cup) of the cooking liquid.

Meanwhile, heat the olive oil in a small frying pan and cook the garlic until golden. Add the pimentón along with the reserved cooking liquid and boil for about 1 minute.

Serve 2 potato halves, half an onion and a portion of fish per plate with a little of the garlic and pimentón sauce poured over the top.

PARGO CON CALABACÍN, ESPINACA Y ACEITUNAS

RED SNAPPER WITH COURGETTE, SPINACH AND OLIVES

I eat this for dinner at least once a month. It's easy to make, with ingredients you can find in any supermarket, and it's quick and healthy! And, let's face it, I love fish above anything else.

Serves 4

2 x 500g (1lb 2oz) red snappers (or any other fish)

4 tbsp olive oil, plus a drizzle

2 pinches of rock or sea salt

4 garlic cloves, thinly sliced

a handful pitted black olives, halved

1 courgette (zucchini), about 200g (7oz), diced

1 tsp sweet pimentón (sweet smoked paprika)

a handful frozen peas, defrosted

3 tbsp sherry vinegar

100g (2 cups) baby spinach

2 tbsp finely chopped fresh chives

salt and freshly ground black pepper

Ask your fishmonger to gut and scale your fish. At home, just wash them in cold water and pat them dry really well with a clean dish cloth or paper towels.

Place a pan wide enough to hold both entire fish over a medium heat. Drizzle over some olive oil, season both sides of the fish with the salt and pan-fry for about 5 minutes on each side, or until crispy and fully cooked. If you put a lid over the pan it will create an oven so that the fish cooks all over and not just on the sides in contact with the pan. Just leave a little opening so that the steam can escape and doesn't condensate on the lid and fall back into the pan, stopping the fish from crisping up properly.

Meanwhile, heat the 4 tablespoons oil in a large frying pan over a high heat. Add the garlic and cook until starting to turn golden, then add the olives and cook for 30 seconds before adding the diced courgette. Fry for 1 minute and then add the sweet pimentón and the peas. Give the pan a good shake and, after 30 seconds, pour over the sherry vinegar and let it reduce for a few seconds. Add the baby spinach and season with salt and pepper, then add the chives.

Serve the fish whole on a warmed platter with the vegetables spooned over the top.

BACALAO Y GAMBAS AL AZAFRÁN CON QUINOA

COD, PRAWNS AND QUINOA WITH SAFFRON SAUCE

Serves 4

16 whole large prawns (jumbo shrimp)
olive oil, for frying
½ onion, thinly sliced
½ leek, thinly sliced
4 garlic cloves, thinly sliced
1g (2 tsp) saffron threads
1 tsp sweet pimentón (sweet smoked paprika)
1 tbsp tomato purée (paste)
1½ tbsp brandy
100ml (scant ½ cup) white wine
200g (7oz) quinoa, rinsed
200ml (scant 1 cup) single (light) cream
4 x 150g (5½oz) cod loins
salt and ground white pepper

Every time I use the head and shells of prawns to make a shellfish stock for a dish, I know that the end result is going to have a refined taste, whether it's a seafood paella or a fish stew.

Peel the prawns and keep the heads and shells for the stock. Set aside the tails. Pour a small drizzle of olive oil into a medium pan over a high heat and fry the heads and shells of the prawns for 5 minutes, or until golden, stirring constantly so that they cook on all sides, then pour in 1 litre (4¾ cups) water. Bring to the boil and cook for 20 minutes, then blend with a hand blender for 20 seconds to squeeze as much flavour from the heads as possible. Pass through a fine sieve and set aside.

Pour 5 tablespoons of oil into a large frying pan over a medium heat and sweat the onion and leek for 15 minutes. Add the garlic and fry over a high heat for 3 minutes, then add the saffron, sweet pimentón and tomato purée. Cook for 2 minutes, then flambé with the brandy followed by the white wine. To do this, slowly tilt the pan towards the flame until the brandy catches, or light with a match. Let the flames flare up then die down.

Add the quinoa to the pan, season and pour over the reserved prawn stock. Cook over a low heat for about 20 minutes, or until the quinoa is tender. Add the cream and prawn tails, stir and bring back to the boil. Cook for 3 minutes, taking care not to overcook the prawns. Meanwhile, pour a little olive oil into a separate pan over a high heat. Season the cod and fry, skin side down, until cooked – 5–10 minutes depending on the thickness. If really thick, carefully turn them over after 5 minutes so that they cook on both sides.

Lay a bed of saffron quinoa on each plate and top with the cod loins and prawns.

ATÚN CON TOMATE
TUNA IN TOMATO SAUCE

Serves 4

4 tbsp olive oil

1 large onion, diced

1 green romano or bell pepper, sliced

4 garlic cloves, chopped

1 tsp sweet pimentón (sweet smoked paprika)

500g (1lb 2oz) chopped peeled tomatoes (tinned is fine)

1 tsp demerara sugar

½ tsp dried oregano or 2 sprigs fresh oregano

1 bay leaf

4 x 150g (5½oz) tuna loin steaks

salt and ground white pepper

This is one of the recipes my mother cooks at home all the time. She makes a very tasty sauce but, with all respect to my mum, she overcooks the fish in a very old-fashioned way. I don't blame her, that is just how she learned to cook it! This is my fresher and lighter version of this home classic, which I will cook for her soon; let's see what she thinks.

Heat the olive oil in a large saucepan over a medium heat and add the onion, pepper and garlic. Fry for 15 minutes, or until the onion is soft and transparent. Add the sweet pimentón and stir for 15 seconds, then add the tomatoes, sugar, oregano, bay leaf and a little pepper. The sugar will reduce the acidity of the tomato, making a more pleasant sauce. I personally like a sweeter tomato sauce, but that's just me! Cook over a medium heat for at least 20 minutes, or until the sauce has reduced a bit and has a rich consistency.

Cut each tuna steak into 6 pieces, season with a bit of salt and add the pieces to the tomato sauce. Simmer for 3 minutes and serve while the tuna is still pink in the middle.

FISH & SEAFOOD

CARPACCIO DE ATÚN

TUNA CARPACCIO WITH OLIVE, MANGO AND CAPER DRESSING

Serves 4

300g (10½oz) fresh tuna loin, about 4cm (1½in) wide and 20cm (8in) long
1 lemon
½ mango, peeled and diced small
6 pitted black olives, halved
1 fresh red chilli pepper, finely chopped
1 tbsp finely chopped fresh chives
2 tbsp capers, drained
6 tbsp extra virgin olive oil
a few fresh coriander (cilantro) leaves
a pinch of sea salt

In Spain we fish tuna off both the north and south coasts of the peninsula. It is very highly regarded, a real delicacy that's pricey but worth every penny. Whether preserved in a glass jar, stewed or served raw, its particular taste and texture transform any recipe into a treat. On a hot summer's day, this lean dish will bring you a smile.

Cut the tuna into 2 smaller loins about 4cm (1½in) wide and 10cm (4in) long. Heat a dry frying pan over a high heat. When it's very hot, add the tuna and sear very lightly on all sides for about 10 seconds on each side. Wrap in plastic wrap and freeze for 2 hours.

Remove the plastic wrap from the chilled tuna and cut into 5mm (¼in) slices with a sharp knife. Arrange on a plate.

Zest the lemon and then remove the peel and cut the flesh into small cubes. Place in a bowl with the mango, olives, chilli pepper and chives. Add the capers and olive oil, mix well and then use to dress the tuna. Garnish with the coriander, season with a bit of salt and enjoy.

MERLUZA A LA ROMANA

HAKE A LA ROMANA WITH MAYONNAISE

'A la romana' is how we define our batter, which is traditionally used for fish but is also used to coat squid or chicken. So, as in the UK, we also coat fish and fry it, however our batter is lighter, as you will see in this recipe. I have a feeling this is the most used technique for cooking fish all over Spain. Every mother of every friend I know cooks fish this way and mine does too. It's as easy as it gets. It is a delicious way to prepare fish because it gets perfectly cooked inside and is not at all heavy, unless you use fries as a garnish! The mayonnaise is just the perfect match.

Serves 2 as a main or 4 as a tapa

100ml (scant ½ cup) olive oil

100ml (scant ½ cup) sunflower oil

100g (¾ cup) plain (all-purpose) flour

1 egg, beaten

2 skinless hake steaks, each weighing about 175g (6oz)

salt

lemon wedges and grated zest, to serve

Mayonnaise (see page 27), to serve

Mix the oils together in a frying pan and place over a medium heat. The oil should not be too hot or it will burn the batter.

Spread out the flour on a plate. Tip the beaten egg into a shallow bowl.

Season the fish with a little salt. If you are going to serve it as a tapa, cut it into bite-sized pieces or goujons. Coat the pieces in the flour, shake off the excess and immediately place it in the beaten egg to coat it well. Shake again to remove the excess and submerge in the hot oil. The oil should sizzle gently. Cook for 5 minutes and then turn the fish and cook for another 3 minutes or so, depending on the size, until golden. Set aside on paper towels to drain the excess oil.

Serve with the lemon wedges, mayonnaise and a sprinkling of lemon zest alongside a fresh salad; try any one from the salad chapter in this book!

Easy tip
After you have finished frying the fish, pour the leftover egg (which will have bits of flour in it) into the hot oil and fry it. We call this *'huevo tonto'*, which translates literally as 'silly egg'.

MEJILLONES EN VINAGRETA

MUSSELS IN A VEGETABLE AND TOMATO VINAIGRETTE

Serves 5 as a tapa

2 large, ripe tomatoes

½ red romano or (bell) pepper, finely chopped

½ green romano or (bell) pepper, finely chopped

1 small onion or a bunch of spring onions (scallions), finely chopped

6 tbsp extra virgin olive oil

3 tbsp sherry vinegar

1 tsp salt

1kg (2lb 3oz) mussels, cleaned and any open or damaged shells discarded

250ml (generous 1 cup) white wine

1 bay leaf

This summery tapas dish is so refreshing and so easy to make that it is almost impossible to fail. These days it can be seen as old fashioned and I don't see it as much as I would like in typical Spanish bars any more. Well, I will be having it on my table every summer, even if it has gone out of fashion!

Cut a cross into the bottom of each tomato with a sharp knife and put them in a pan of boiling water for a few seconds. Remove from the water and let cool a little, then peel and cut each one into 4 wedges. Remove the seeds and discard, then cut the tomato flesh into small cubes. This method of preparation is called a tomato concasse.

Mix together the chopped tomatoes, peppers and onion with the oil, sherry vinegar and salt. Set aside.

Make sure your mussels are well cleaned. Use a knife to remove the filaments and any barnacles left on the shells as they will be part of the final presentation.

Put 500ml (2 cups) water and the wine in a deep pan with the bay leaf and bring it to the boil, then add the clean mussels, cover and cook for about 3 minutes, or until they open. Remove the mussels from the water and set aside to cool. Add 1 tablespoon of the cooking water to the vinaigrette to enhance the mussel flavour.

Once the mussels have cooled a little, separate the shells and the meat attached and mix this mussel meat with the vinaigrette.

There are many ways to serve this tapa. My favourite is to lay half the shells on a tray and spoon 1 mussel with a bit of sauce into each one. Alternatively, serve over warm buttered toast, gem lettuce leaves... the possibilities are endless.

Easy tip
Don't pour away the cooking liquor from boilind the mussels! Use it as a fish stock or in a paella.

BERBERECHOS AL FINO

COCKLES IN A DRY SHERRY SAUCE

Serves 2

4 tbsp extra virgin olive oil

2 garlic cloves, finely chopped

1 cayenne chilli pepper, finely chopped

1 slice Serrano ham, finely chopped

500g (1lb 2oz) cockles, cleaned and any open or damaged shells discarded

1½ tbsp fino sherry

2 tbsp finely chopped fresh parsley

salt and freshly ground black pepper

In Spain, anything with two shells we just love, as long as it comes with a lovely sauce we can mop up with bread when the plate is finished.

Pour the olive oil into a small frying pan over a high heat and fry the garlic, chilli and Serrano ham until golden.

Add the cockles to the pan, season with salt and pepper and pour over the fino sherry. Cover and let the cockles steam for about 2 minutes.

Sprinkle with the finely chopped parsley and serve.

Easy swap
This dish works equally well with any other shellfish, such as mussels or clams. Use what is in season and at its best.

FISH & SEAFOOD

ALMEJAS A LA MARINERA

FISHERMAN-STYLE CLAMS

This dish relies on little more than fresh clams as this is how fishermen would cook them while out on the boat. But it's just as popular on land!

Serves 4 as a tapa

600g (1lb 5oz) clams, cleaned and any open or damaged shells discarded

4 tbsp extra virgin olive oil

½ onion, finely chopped

2 garlic cloves, finely chopped

¼ red chilli pepper, finely chopped

2 tsp plain (all-purpose) flour

1 tsp sweet pimentón (sweet smoked paprika)

1 tsp salt

160ml (⅔ cup) white wine

2 tbsp finely chopped fresh parsley

Put the clams in a large bowl or in the sink, cover with cold salty water and leave for 1 hour, moving them around with your hand from time to time. This will help the clams to open and release any sand.

Place a large frying pan over a high heat and add the oil, onion, garlic and chilli and cook until the onion is transparent and soft, about 10 minutes. Reduce the heat and add the flour, pimentón and salt, stirring continuously for 1 minute to cook the flour and make a roux.

Add the wine, little by little, stirring vigorously until the wine and flour are completely combined. Continue to cook for at least 2 minutes over a low heat. If you see that the sauce is getting too thick, add a bit of water. Drain the clams and add them to the pan with the parsley, stir thoroughly, cover and cook for another 2 minutes.

Remove the lid and toss the mixture a few times. By now, all the clams should be open; if not, cover and cook for another minute or so. Discard any clams that do not open before serving.

MEJILLONES A LA CREMA

MUSSELS IN A CREAM SAUCE

The vast majority of the mussels we eat in Spain come from the Galician *rías* (similar to fjords), cultivated in vast quantities to satisfy Spanish demand. It is also in the north of Spain that you will find most of Spain's dairy products because as well as having wild seas, there is very wet weather that is ideal for cattle farming.

Serves 10

2 sprigs fresh thyme

1 bay leaf

2kg (4½lb) mussels, cleaned and any open or damaged shells discarded

olive oil, for frying

1 bunch spring onions (scallions), finely chopped

350ml (1½ cups) white wine

200ml (scant 1 cup) single (light) cream

1 tbsp cornflour (cornstarch), optional

salt and freshly ground black pepper

Place the thyme and bay leaf in a deep pan with 500ml (2 cups) water, set over a high heat and bring to the boil. Add the mussels, cover and cook for about 3 minutes, or until the mussels are just opened. Remove and set aside, discarding any that haven't opened. Reserve the cooking water.

Remove the bay leaf and thyme from the water and boil over a high heat until the liquid has reduced by half. Set aside.

Pour a drizzle of olive oil into a saucepan over a low heat and fry the spring onions until soft, about 10 minutes. Add the wine, turn up the heat and boil for about 1 minute to make sure most of the alcohol has evaporated, then add the reserved cooking water from the mussels. Continue to boil for 6 minutes, then season with salt and pepper and pour in the cream. Reduce the heat to low. If the sauce is too thin, continue to cook for another 6 minutes to thicken it, or dilute the cornflour in cold water and stir it into the sauce.

Add the mussels and mix with the cream sauce to warm them through before serving.

Easy tip
To minimize splashing when you add the mussels to the hot water, put them in a bowl first and add them to the water in one go.

CALAMARES EN SU TINTA

SQUID IN BLACK INK SAUCE

Unfortunately, outside the Mediterranean and Asia squid is only popular as fried rings. I sometimes wonder if people believe that squid are actually rings that swim in the sea! In Spain we cook squid in many different ways and it's a fundamental ingredient in so many recipes. In this one it's all about the depth of flavour because to me, if there is a flavour of the sea it is in squid ink. I consider this dish to be a showstopper and it's not just because of the colour!

Serves 6

- 1kg (2lb 3oz) fresh squid or baby squid, cleaned (ask your fishmonger to do this for you)
- 6 or 7 slices stale hard white bread such as ciabatta or baguette
- 185ml (¾ cup) white wine
- 6 x 4g (about 1½ tbsp in total) sachets squid ink (ask your fishmonger)
- 5 tbsp olive oil
- 3 medium onions, roughly chopped
- 1 small carrot, roughly chopped
- 2 garlic cloves, finely chopped
- 1 bay leaf
- 200ml (scant 1 cup) tomato passata (or strained or milled tinned tomatoes)
- 185ml (¾ cup) fish stock or water
- salt and freshly ground black pepper

Cut the squid tubes into rings and set aside with the tentacles. If you have baby squid, stuff the tentacles inside the tubes and close with a toothpick.

Toast the bread and then place it in a mixing bowl with the white wine and the squid ink. Set aside.

Pour the olive oil into a deep pan. Set over a medium heat and add the chopped vegetables, garlic and bay leaf and fry slowly for about 8 minutes or until the onions look transparent. Add the passata, reduce the heat to low and cook for another 2 minutes, stirring continuously with a wooden spoon to stop the sauce from catching.

Add the inky bread and the fish stock, season with salt and pepper and cook over a low heat for another 15 minutes before blending with a stick blender to make a thick, shiny black sauce with reddish hints. If it is too thick you can add some more water or fish stock.

Finally, add the squid to the sauce and cook for 20 minutes, or until the squid is soft.

SEPIA A LA PLANCHA CON AJILIMÓJILI
GRILLED CUTTLEFISH

If you ask anyone in Spain for 'sepia a la plancha', or grilled cuttlefish, it will bring back memories of moments at *chiringuitos*, or beach huts, with family or friends. Instead of having this dish in a fancy restaurant, it's best to have it at a traditional al fresco beach bar. The trick is definitely in the olive oil with the garlic and parsley – I'm sure you will get it right. It couldn't be any easier to make at home.

Serves 2

1 tbsp chopped flat-leaf parsley
2 garlic cloves, finely chopped
4 tbsp olive oil, plus extra for drizzling
1 cuttlefish (about 500g/1lb 2oz), cleaned (ask your fishmonger to do this for you)
1 heaped tbsp rock or sea salt
lemon wedges, to serve

In a bowl, mix together the parsley, garlic and olive oil.

It is important to prepare the cuttlefish before cooking, otherwise it will be tough and won't cook evenly. Make sure you remove all the layers of skin until there is only white flesh and then, with a sharp knife, score the inside of the body in a cross-hatch pattern.

To cook 'a la plancha' requires a very hot pan, as hot as it can get. Place a large, dry frying pan over a high heat. While the pan is getting hot, sprinkle the salt over the surface. When you can feel the heat over the pan, place the cuttlefish on top of the salt and drizzle it with a little olive oil.

After 2 minutes, drizzle the cuttlefish with 2 tablespoons of the prepared parsley oil and turn it over. Be aware that it will smoke a lot and this will give the fish a 'plancha-style' aroma. Cook for at least another 2 minutes, depending on the size of the cuttlefish.

Chop into bite-sized chunks and pour over the remaining parsley oil. Serve with lemon wedges.

SEPIA CON SOBRASADA O CHORIZO

CUTTLEFISH WITH SOBRASADA SAUSAGE OR CHORIZO

This stew is not very well known in mainland Spain, however it is a typical dish in the Balearic Islands, specifically in Mallorca, where the traditional Sobrasada sausage comes from. This product is very special; if I had to describe it it would be as a chorizo pâté. Cuttlefish is soft and delicate and therefore quick and easy to cook, making this delicious dish really simple to make.

Serves 4

1 medium to large cuttlefish, cleaned (ask your fishmonger to do this for you)

olive oil, for frying

1 onion, finely chopped

2 bay leaves

130g (4½oz) Sobrasada de Mallorca or cured chorizo sausage, chopped small

200ml (scant 1 cup) white wine

150g (heaped ½ cup) tomato passata (or strained or milled tinned tomatoes)

Cut the cleaned cuttlefish into small pieces about 2.5cm (1in) wide.

Heat some olive oil in a medium-sized pan over a medium heat and sauté the onion with the bay leaves. If you are using chorizo sausage, this would be the time to add it. Once the onion is transparent and soft, add the cuttlefish pieces, stir once and immediately pour over the wine. Cook over a high heat for at least 1 minute, until some of the alcohol has evaporated, then add the passata and cook for a further 3 minutes.

Using your hands, soften the Sobrasada, if using, and add it to the stew. Keep stirring to make sure all the ingredients are well mixed and cook for a further 2 minutes, then serve.

Easy swap
Sobrasada sausage can be found online, but if you can't get hold of any, blend some chorizo into a paste with a drizzle of olive oil in a food processor.

VIEIRAS GRATINADAS

SCALLOP AND SERRANO HAM GRATIN SERVED IN A SHELL

I've noticed that scallops are more common in the UK than they are in Spain. I can see them in almost any restaurant and the variations are endless. In my country we don't eat them that much. This is perhaps because we have a larger variety of other seafood available. Having said that, this recipe carries a flavour punch. For those who hate anchovies, don't let the anchovy in the breadcrumbs put you off; trust me when I say that after cooking the anchovy will not taste anything like it does when you take it out of the tin.

Serves 4 as a tapa

8 scallops in their shells (you can ask your fishmonger to open them for you)

275ml (1 cup + 2½ tbsp) whole milk

30g (2 tbsp) butter

¼ onion, finely chopped

30g (1oz) Serrano ham, finely chopped

30g (2 tbsp) plain (all-purpose) flour

a pinch of salt

a pinch of white pepper

4 tbsp breadcrumbs

1 salted anchovy

1 sprig fresh parsley

Open the scallops and use a sharp knife to separate the meat from the shell. Scrap any ugly bits so that you're left with the white meat and the red roe. If you don't like the roe, just remove it. Wash the shells and scallops, pat dry with paper towels and set aside.

Warm the milk in a small pan over a low heat. Preheat the grill (broiler) to hot.

Melt the butter in a medium pan over a medium heat and fry the onion and ham for a few minutes until the onion is soft and transparent. Add the flour and cook for 5 more minutes, stirring continuously, until the flour has a light toasted colour. Add the warmed milk, little by little, and the salt and pepper, stirring all the time until you have a smooth and silky white béchamel sauce. Lower the heat and simmer for about 15 minutes, stirring so that the sauce doesn't stick to the pan.

Tip the breadcrumbs, anchovy and parsley into a food processor and blend.

Line up the shells on a baking sheet and place a scallop on each shell. Cover with a couple of spoonfuls of the ham béchamel and sprinkle over the anchovy breadcrumbs. Grill for 5 minutes and serve hot.

huevos y aves
EGGS & POULTRY

HUEVOS A LA FLAMENCA

BAKED EGGS WITH HAM IN TOMATO SAUCE

This traditional Andalusian dish can be prepared in a snip and is ideal for chucking in whatever ingredients you happen to have in the fridge – plenty of veggies, a bit of ham (bacon or chorizo) and eggs. Just a few staples thrown together.

Serves 4 as a tapa

300g (2 cups fresh or 2½ cups frozen) peas

300g (10½oz) asparagus or 1 red or green (bell) pepper, chopped

3½ tbsp olive oil

2 garlic cloves, thinly sliced

1 medium onion, finely chopped

4 slices Serrano ham or 1 chorizo sausage, chopped

1 x 400g (14oz) tin chopped (diced) tomatoes

a pinch of sugar

½ tsp sweet pimentón (sweet smoked paprika)

½ tsp hot pimentón (hot smoked paprika)

1 tbsp finely chopped fresh parsley, plus a little extra to garnish

4 eggs (or 8 if you are really hungry)

salt and freshly ground black pepper

bread, to serve

Preheat the oven to 180°C/160°C fan/350°F/gas mark 4.

Prepare a saucepan with boiling water and add the peas, asparagus and a pinch of salt. Boil for 2 minutes, then drain and rinse with cold water to stop the vegetables from cooking. Set aside.

Put the olive oil in a frying pan over a medium heat. Add the garlic and fry for a few seconds before adding the chopped onion and the ham or chorizo. Cook for about 5 minutes and then add the asparagus and peas. Cook for a further 5 minutes before adding the chopped tomatoes, sugar, sweet pimentón, hot pimentón and a pinch of salt (don't over-season at this point as the ham or chorizo will release more salt when baking). Cook it for 10 minutes over a low heat. Add the parsley.

Pour into a medium ovenproof dish or 4 individual dishes, crack the eggs over the top and season. Bake for 7–8 minutes, or until the egg is cooked to your liking. Garnish with a little finely chopped fresh parsley and serve with good bread.

Note
Duck eggs work really well in this dish; they have that extra bit of flavour and, as we know, size does matter.

REVUELTO DE SETAS

SCRAMBLED EGGS WITH WILD MUSHROOMS

Scrambled eggs is a star dish for a weekend breakfast for most people in the UK; in Spain we prefer to have it for dinner (I prefer churros for breakfast). We add more ingredients, such as mushrooms, spinach or even prawns (shrimp), and that is what boosts a nutritional dinner and makes the eggs into something a bit more filling.

Serves 2

a drizzle of olive oil

1 small chilli or cayenne pepper, finely chopped

200g (3 cups) wild mushrooms or a mixture of oyster and shiitake, chopped

2 garlic cloves, sliced

4 eggs

salt and freshly ground black pepper

Heat the olive oil in a frying pan over a medium heat and fry the chopped chilli pepper for 30 seconds. Add the mushrooms and a pinch of salt and sauté for 3–4 minutes. Add the sliced garlic and fry for a couple more minutes.

Crack all the eggs on top of the mushrooms and stir together until the eggs look smooth and are still runny. I do not recommend beating the eggs first. Remove from the heat – the remaining heat will keep the eggs cooking until they're done. Season with salt and black pepper and serve.

TORTILLA FRANCESA
NOT JUST ANOTHER FRENCH OMLETTE

What if I told you that I was taught how to make this French omelette while working for the famous chef Ferran Adrià, and that I promise to you I have never tried a French omelette this good in my life – would that be enough to catch your attention with such a simple dish? Next time you need to cook an omelette, do me a favour and remember you read this, then read it again and try it.

Serves 1

3 organic, free-range eggs
1 tsp extra virgin olive oil
a pinch of salt

Crack the eggs into a bowl, making sure there is no shell in it. Whisk lightly with a fork for no longer than 30 seconds.

Place a large, non-stick frying pan over a low-medium heat. Pour the olive oil into the pan and use folded paper towels to spread the oil all over the surface, coating every single corner of it. Be careful not to burn the tips of your fingers.

The pan shouldn't be too hot. This is one of the keys to a great omelette, which should cook slowly and in layers, like crêpes.

Sprinkle the salt into the eggs and whisk for 5 more seconds, then pour them into the pan.

After 10 seconds, and with the help of a flexible spatula, fold one side into the other to form a half-moon shape. Tilt the pan over the empty half so that it fills with runny egg again to form another layer. Fold the other half into the newly forming layer and tilt the pan over the empty side to fill it again and form another layer.

Turn off the heat so that the last 2 layers cook with the residual heat. Just repeat the process as many or as few times as needed until there is no runny egg remaining to coat the pan when you tilt it.

Fold the omelette and enjoy right away.

HUEVOS CON CHORIZO BENEDICTINOS

EGGS BENEDICT WITH SPINACH AND CHORIZO HOLLANDAISE

Eggs Benedict are unbeatable, the perfect brunch to me. Not Spanish at all, but when I made the chorizo hollandaise for the first time I swear I thought I had just changed the world forever. I thought to myself 'I have just brought eggs Benedict to a whole other level'. I was full of pride. I don't want to sound arrogant but, honestly, my weekend mornings haven't been the same again since.

Serves 4

2 cooking chorizo (fresh uncooked) sausages (preferably lightly smoked), finely chopped

200g (scant 1 cup) unsalted butter

4–8 eggs, plus 2 yolks

juice from ½ lemon

2 tbsp extra virgin olive oil

1 garlic clove, finely chopped

250g (4½ cups) baby spinach

salt and freshly ground black pepper

4 slices toasted brioche, to serve

sweet pimentón (sweet smoked paprika), to serve

Heat a frying pan over a medium heat and dry-fry the chorizo for 3–4 minutes. Add the butter and melt.

Pour a few inches of water into a small saucepan over a medium heat. Put the 5 egg yolks, lemon juice, 2 tablespoons water and a pinch of salt into a heatproof bowl slightly larger than the saucepan. Rest the bowl over the saucepan and whisk the egg yolk mixture for about 2 minutes, or until it gets fluffy, taking care not to overcook it. While whisking, slowly add the chorizo butter in a thin stream until the sauce has fully emulsified and has a creamy mayonnaise texture. Add a touch of salt and pepper and set aside.

Heat the oil in a pan over a medium heat and fry the garlic for a few seconds before adding the baby spinach. Cook for 1 minute to allow the spinach leaves to wilt. Season with salt and pepper and set aside.

Lay the toasted brioche slices on serving plates and top each with a spoonful of spinach.

One at a time, break each egg into a ramekin and pour into a pan of simmering water. Gently poach for 2–3 minutes, remove with a slotted spoon and place 1 or 2 eggs on top of each brioche slice. To finish, spoon the warm chorizo hollandaise over the poached eggs and sprinkle pimentón over each one.

EGGS & POULTRY

ALITAS DE POLLO A LA MIEL Y LIMÓN

HONEY AND LEMON CHICKEN WINGS

I am yet to meet someone who doesn't like chicken wings. Traditionally this recipe was made using the whole chicken, however it is so much more shareable when made with wings.

Serves 4

400g (14oz) chicken wings

1 lemon

3 tbsp extra virgin olive oil

4 sprigs fresh thyme

1 head of garlic, cut in half horizontally

a pinch of sweet pimentón (sweet smoked paprika)

3 tbsp honey

2 tbsp chopped fresh coriander (cilantro) leaves

sea salt and freshly ground black pepper

Bring a pan of water to the boil, add the chicken wings and boil for 5 minutes. Remove and drain on paper towels for 5 minutes.

Meanwhile, zest the lemon, halve it and squeeze out the juice, but don't throw the rest of it away.

Heat the oil in a frying pan over a high heat. Add the thyme sprigs, chicken wings, squeezed lemon halves and the garlic and fry for a couple of minutes on each side. Sprinkle the pimentón over the chicken and after 10 seconds drizzle the lemon juice and honey into the pan. Season with salt and pepper.

Continue to sauté the chicken until cooked through, allowing the liquid to reduce while making sure the wings are fully coated in the glaze. Add the lemon zest right at the end as it turns bitter if added too early and loses its fragrance quite quickly.

Sprinkle with the chopped coriander and sea salt before serving.

POLLASTRE AL AST

SPANISH STYLE ROAST CHICKEN

This is proper street food for us in Spain. You will find the biggest rotisseries I've ever seen in street-food markets across the country on the weekends, packed with beautifully golden and crispy little chickens, intoxicating the markets with their beautiful aroma. It is always the last stop before you go home after your grocery shopping. Simplicity at its best and so easy to make at home.

Serves 2

1 small free-range chicken
2 tbsp lard or olive oil
1 tsp salt
2 generous pinches of black pepper
2 tbsp herbes de Provence

Preheat the oven to 200°C/180°C fan/400°F/gas mark 6.

Rub the entire chicken, inside and out, with the lard. Season with the salt, black pepper and herbs, again inside and outside.

Fill an tall, empty can such as a beer can with water and stand it in the middle of a roasting tray. Stand the chicken on the can, inserting it into the cavity, so that the wings point up and the drumsticks hang down. This will allow air to circulate around the chicken.

Place the tray on the lowest rack of the oven and cook for 20 minutes, then reduce the heat to 160°C/140°C fan/325°F/gas mark 3 and cook for a further 45 minutes, or until ready. The skin should be very crispy but the meat should still be very moist inside, with the juices running clear.

PINCHOS DE POLLO

MARINATED CHICKEN SKEWERS

The best thing about these skewers is that they can be prepared well in advance if you are making a BBQ, so there will be no hassle when you fire up the grill. They can, of course, be cooked in the oven, too, as here.

Serves 4

600g (1lb 5oz) boneless and skinless chicken thighs

3 sprigs fresh coriander (cilantro), finely chopped

1 garlic clove, finely chopped

4 tbsp olive oil

1 tbsp honey

grated zest and juice of 1 lemon

1 tbsp sweet pimentón (sweet smoked paprika)

1 tsp ground turmeric

1 tsp ground cumin

a pinch of ground black pepper

12 x 18cm (7in) wooden skewers, soaked in water for 10 minutes

Cut each chicken thigh into 6 even-sized pieces and place in a non-metallic bowl.

Mix together all the rest of the ingredients to make a marinade and pour over the chicken. Mix it all together, cover with plastic wrap and leave to marinate in the fridge for at least 30 minutes or up to 3 days.

Preheat the oven to 200°C/180°C fan/400°F/gas mark 6.

Thread 6 pieces of chicken onto each skewer and season generously with salt.

Roast for about 10 minutes, or until cooked through.

Easy swap
You can of course replace the chicken thighs in this recipe with pork, lamb, turkey or whichever meat you prefer.

CODORNICES CON ROMESCO

SPATCHCOCK QUAIL WITH ROMESCO SAUCE

Serves 4

4 quail
1 lemon, quartered, to serve

For the romesco sauce
3 pimientos choriceros (Spanish dried peppers), chopped, optional
1 red (bell) pepper
3 tomatoes
½ head of garlic, peeled and cloves separated
100ml (scant ½ cup) olive oil
50g (heaped ⅓ cup) blanched almonds (or skin on)
30g (¼ cup) blanched hazelnuts (or pine nuts or more almonds)
1 slice rustic bread
3 tbsp sherry vinegar
a pinch of sweet pimentón (sweet smoked paprika)
a pinch of rock or sea salt

For the marinade
10 sprigs fresh thyme, leaves finely chopped
4 garlic cloves, finely chopped
1 tbsp salt
2 tsp sweet or hot pimentón (sweet or hot smoked paprika)
2 tsp dried oregano
2 tsp ground cumin
5 tbsp olive oil

It is generally when the sun is out that spatchcocking comes in handy to get perfectly cooked birds, and this dish is ideal cooked over a BBQ, although it's just as good under the grill (broiler). This recipe and the accompanying sauce will be a great addition to your summer grilling repertoire.

Soak the pimientos choriceros (if using) in water for 2 hours.

Preheat the oven to 200°C/180°C fan/400°F/gas mark 6.

Tip the vegetables for the romesco sauce onto a roasting tray and rub with the olive oil. Roast for 25 minutes, adding the nuts and the slice of bread for the last 10 minutes of cooking. Set aside to cool slightly and then remove the skins from the vegetables and blend with the bread, nuts, sherry vinegar, pimentón, salt and pimientos choriceros, if using (by pestle, hand blender or food processor) until you have a smooth paste.

Lay a quail on a chopping board and use a sharp knife to cut the rib cage wide open. Discard the chest bone, flip over the quail and flatten it against the board. Insert 2 skewers diagonally in a cross formation from the wing to the leg, passing through the breast so that you have a completely flat bird. Repeat with the rest of the quail.

Mix together the marinade ingredients and brush all over the quail.

Preheat the grill (broiler) or BBQ to hot or place a ridged griddle pan over a high heat and cook the quail to your liking, no longer than 5 minutes on each side and ideally so that it is cooked through but still juicy in the middle.

Serve each of the quail with a lemon wedge and a spoonful of romesco sauce.

Easy tip
Romesco can also be enjoyed with grilled or boiled veg or pan-fried fish.

PATO CON CIRUELAS

DUCK WITH PRUNES, CHESTNUTS AND PEDRO XIMÉNEZ SHERRY

This dish has all the elements of the perfect Christmas centrepiece, if it wasn't for the fact that it is just too easy to prepare. You know how complicated we like to make it when it comes to Christmas – nothing can take half an hour.

Serves 6

3 tbsp olive oil

1 small whole duck (about 1.5kg/3lb 5oz), oven-ready

8 garlic cloves, skin on but crushed

a handful of peeled chestnuts

1 onion, thinly sliced

6 sprigs fresh thyme

12 prunes

125ml (½ cup) sweet Pedro Ximénez sherry

salt and freshly ground black pepper

bread or roasted new potatoes, to serve

Preheat the oven to 200°C/180°C fan/400°F/gas mark 6.

Heat the olive oil in a wide ovenproof pan or casserole dish over a medium heat. Season the duck with salt and pepper and pan-fry on all sides until golden. Help yourself with a pair of tongs. After 10 minutes, remove the duck from the pan and set aside.

Add the garlic cloves, chestnuts and onion to the pan and fry for 10 minutes. Add the thyme and prunes and cook for a further 5 minutes. Return the duck to the pan and pour over the sherry, then add 250ml (generous 1 cup) water.

Put the pan in the oven and cook for 25 minutes, then switch off the heat and leave the duck in the oven for a further 20 minutes without opening the door. This should crisp up the skin and cook the duck to perfection as well as resting the meat.

Serve as a centrepiece with some good bread or roasted new potatoes.

Easy tip
For a really delicious accompaniment, cook the duck sitting over 600g (1lb 5oz) new potatoes so that the potatoes roast in the sauce and meat juices.

verduras
VEGETABLES

ESPÁRRAGOS CON JAMÓN
GREEN ASPARAGUS WITH SERRANO HAM

When asparagus is in season, it's a big event every year. Everyone promotes it with pride, whether on the supermarket shelves or high up on restaurant menus. It is a very special veggie to me. I love its flavour and versatility, since it just goes well with so many other foods. In Spain it's very common to find it served with ham – simple and delicious.

Serves 3 as a tapa

1 bunch green asparagus

a drizzle of olive oil

2 garlic cloves, thinly sliced

2 slices Serrano ham, chopped, plus 1 slice to serve

a pinch of sea salt

a pinch of freshly ground black pepper

1½ tbsp dry sherry wine or a splash of sherry vinegar

50g (2oz) Manchego cheese, sliced

Snap off the hard ends of the asparagus and blanch the spears for 2 minutes in a pan of boiling water. Depending on the thickness of the asparagus you may need a bit longer to get them cooked.

Heat the oil in a frying pan over a medium heat and cook the garlic and the chopped ham until the garlic is golden. Add the blanched asparagus, season with the salt and pepper and sauté for 30 seconds, then flambé with the dry sherry wine. To do this, slowly tilt the pan towards the flame until the wine catches, or light with a match. Let the flames flare up then die down. Serve with the sliced Manchego and a slice of ham.

Note
If you ever come across fresh Spanish white asparagus in a market, please buy them. They are very temperamental and need to be very fresh or they get tough and bitter. But young and fresh they are a real treat. You can make this dish with white asparagus by boiling them for at least 10 minutes longer than green ones with a tablespoon of sugar and a knob of butter in the water.

ACELGAS CON PATATAS

SWISS CHARD WITH POTATOES

This is a healthy dish for a nutritious supper. In Spain we often use chard as it is less sweet than spinach and works well with the potatoes. You can use any kind of chard – if you can find them with red, white or yellow stems you can mix them and create a more colourful plate.

Serves 24

2 bunches Swiss chard (about 10 leaves), washed

4 waxy potatoes, peeled and quartered

For the sofrito de ajo dressing

4 tbsp extra virgin olive oil

4 garlic cloves, sliced

1 tsp sweet pimentón (sweet smoked paprika)

3 tbsp sherry vinegar

Trim the stems from the chard leaves and slice thinly. Cut the leaves into strips.

Bring a large pan of salted water to the boil over a high heat and cook the potatoes for 12 minutes, or until soft but still undercooked. Add the chard stems and cook for a further 5 minutes before adding the leaves. Cook for another 3 minutes.

Drain the vegetables in a colander. Don't worry if the potatoes break or mash – if they are good waxy potatoes this will add a fantastic texture to the greens.

For the sofrito de ajo dressing, heat the olive oil in a large frying pan over a medium heat and cook the garlic until golden. Take the pan off the heat and add the pimentón, give it a good stir and add the sherry vinegar before pouring this sofrito over the potatoes and chard. Mix well and serve.

PIQUILLOS RELLENOS DE SETAS

PIQUILLO PEPPERS STUFFED WITH MUSHROOMS

I have always been a big fan of mushrooms in all their forms – from taking long walks with family to pick wild mushrooms, to cooking them in many ways at home. This recipe is packed full of tastiness.

Serves 6 as a tapa

- 150g (5oz) wild mushrooms, such as oyster, or a mixture of field mushrooms
- 3½ tbsp olive oil
- ¼ small onion, finely chopped
- 2 garlic cloves, finely chopped
- 2 sprigs fresh thyme
- a splash of white wine
- 30g (2 tbsp) butter
- 50g (3⅔ tbsp) plain (all-purpose) flour
- 400ml (1¾ cups) whole milk, hot
- a pinch of grated nutmeg
- 15 tinned piquillo peppers
- 400ml (1¾ cups) double (heavy) cream
- 50g (½ cup) grated cheddar cheese, plus extra for topping
- salt and freshly ground black pepper
- bread, to serve

Trim the mushrooms, removing the stalks, and wipe them with a damp cloth. Roughly chop. Heat the olive oil in a large frying pan over a high heat and fry the mushrooms for at least 2 minutes, season with salt and pepper, stir well and season again. Fry for a further 2 minutes. Add the onion and cook for 1 minute. Add the garlic, thyme and cook for 2 minutes, then add the wine and cook for 1 minute.

Lower the heat to medium and add the butter. Let it melt, then add the flour and cook for 5 minutes, stirring constantly, until the flour is lightly toasted. Add the hot milk, little by little, and the nutmeg, whisking until you have a smooth and silky white sauce. Simmer for about 20 minutes, stirring from time to time to make sure it doesn't catch on the bottom of the pan, until the béchamel sauce has thickened. Pour into a bowl and cover with plastic wrap. Chill completely in the fridge. After at least 2 hours, the béchamel should be firm and ready to handle.

Preheat the oven to 160°C/140°C fan/325°F/gas mark 3.

Bring 3 of the piquillo peppers, the cream and cheese to the boil in a small pan over a medium heat and cook for 10 minutes. Season with salt and pepper. Use a hand blender to blend until smooth.

Using a spoon, fill the remaining 12 piquillo peppers with the mushroom béchamel. Lay them in an oven dish and pour the piquillo sauce on top. Scatter some more grated chese over the top. Bake for 15 minutes until lightly browned and crispy on top. Serve with bread.

Recipe pictured overleaf.

VEGETABLES

BERENJENAS FRITAS CON MIEL

AUBERGINES WITH HONEY

I am sure you'll love this one. In Córdoba and Malaga, southern Spain, this is a classic and whenever I've put it on one of my restaurant menus, everyone has loved it.

Serves 4 as a tapa

1 aubergine (eggplant)
200ml (scant 1 cup) whole milk
2 tbsp dark muscovado sugar
2 tbsp honey
1 egg yolk
1 tbsp lager
2 tbsp plain (all-purpose) flour
1 tsp sea salt
400ml (1¾ cups) sunflower oil, for deep-frying

Cut the aubergine into batons as if they were fat-cut chips (or round slices, half moons... it makes no difference) and place in a bowl. Pour over the milk, completely submerging the aubergine, and set aside for at least 30 minutes. This will remove any sourness from the aubergine.

Melt the muscovado sugar and honey together in a small pan over a low heat for 5 minutes. It doesn't need cooking, just melting.

Meanwhile, beat the egg yolk in a clean mixing bowl until it is soft and airy. Add the beer (I just gave you a reason to drink the rest) and flour, stirring with a whisk to make sure it is all properly mixed. Leave to rest for 15 minutes and then add the salt and stir until it is well combined with the mixture.

Heat the oil in a tall-sided pan over a medium-high heat until a cube of day-old bread dropped into the oil turns golden in about 30 seconds. Alternatively, heat a deep fryer to 180°C (360°F). The oil should not be too hot or smoking.

Drain the aubergine pieces and coat them with the batter mixture. Deep-fry in batches, perhaps 3 or 4 batons at a time, until they have a nice golden colour, and then drain on paper towels.

Serve the aubergine batons with a good drizzle of the muscovado honey over the top.

VEGETABLES

CALABACÍN A LA MALLORQUINA
STUFFED COURGETTES

This is my version of the better-known aubergines Mallorca-style. I've chosen courgettes here instead because I think their meat is more delicate and this complements the heavy meat filling better.

Serves 6

6 large courgettes (zucchini)
olive oil, for frying
1 large onion, finely chopped
4 garlic cloves, crushed
250g (9oz) minced (ground) beef
2 tbsp tomato purée (paste)
3 sprigs fresh thyme
2–3 fresh marjoram leaves (or 1 tsp dried oregano)
330ml (1¼ cups + 2 tbsp) lager
2 tsp cornflour (cornstarch)
1 egg yolk
125ml (½ cup) milk
100g (2 cups) breadcrumbs
salt and freshly ground black pepper

Cut the courgettes in half lengthways and use a spoon to scoop out the flesh. Finely chop the flesh and set it and the halved courgettes aside.

Heat a drizzle of oil in a pan over a medium heat and add the onion, garlic and chopped courgette. Cook until soft and golden, making sure the vegetables don't burn. Add the meat, the tomato purée, salt and pepper, thyme and marjoram and cook for about 10 minutes, stirring vigorously for the first 2 minutes so that the meat breaks up into small pieces. When the meat is cooked through, pour over the lager and let simmer for about 30 minutes, or until the liquid has completely reduced down.

In a bowl, combine the cornflour, egg yolk and the cold milk and beat until the cornflour is diluted. Add this mixture to the meat and stir for 1–2 minutes until the sauce thickens up and then remove from the heat right away.

Preheat the oven to 180°C/160°C fan/350°F/gas mark 4.

Fill the halved courgettes with the meat mixture, sprinkle the breadcrumbs over the top and bake for 20 minutes, or until the breadcrumbs are crisp and golden and the courgette boats have cooked through.

COLIFLOR CON AJOS, VINAGRE Y ALCAPARRAS

CAULIFLOWER WITH GARLIC, VINEGAR AND CAPERS

This takes just 15 minutes to make and I cook it very often at home because it's simple, light and healthy and it's full of flavour. This is a Spanish version of a Chinese stir-fry.

Serves 4 as a tapa

1 large cauliflower, broken into florets and leaves reserved

extra virgin olive oil, for frying

5 garlic cloves, sliced

50g (5 tbsp) drained capers

1 tsp cumin seeds

½ tsp sweet pimentón (sweet smoked paprika)

3½ tbsp sherry or other white vinegar

salt

Place a large pot filled with water over a high heat. Bring to the boil, then add the cauliflower florets and cook for about 4 minutes. Drain then refresh under cold running water. Set aside.

Pour a good drizzle of oil into a cold frying pan, add the reserved cauliflower leaves, sliced garlic, capers and cumin seeds and then turn the heat to high. When the garlic turns golden, add the pimentón and then the sherry vinegar. Reduce the liquid for 30 seconds and then toss the cauliflower into the pan. Make sure the ingredients are well mixed and serve.

HABAS CON CHORIZO

BROAD BEANS WITH CHORIZO

Serves 4 as a tapa

250g (2 cups) shelled broad (fava) beans (if you find baby broad beans, even better)

3½ tbsp extra virgin olive oil

¼ onion, finely chopped

5 garlic cloves, skin on but crushed

1 sprig fresh oregano

1 cooking chorizo (fresh uncooked) sausage (about 90g/3¼oz), chopped

grated zest and juice of ½ lemon

sea salt and freshly ground black pepper

bread, to serve

Broad (fava) beans are widely consumed all over Spain. We love to eat them in many ways: in stews, soups and paellas, or even raw and salted as a snack. The tender seeds within the pod are delicious. The younger they are, the better, but obviously the more expensive, too.

Bring a large pan of salted water to the boil. Add the beans, bring back to the boil and then cook for 2 minutes. Drain and rinse with cold running water. Set aside.

Heat the olive oil in a frying pan over a medium heat and add the onion, garlic, oregano and chorizo. Sweat for 5 minutes, or until the onion is transparent and soft. Increase the heat to high, add the broad beans and sauté for a couple of minutes.

Add 2 tablespoons of water, the lemon zest and juice, season with some salt and pepper and serve with some good bread.

PATATAS MACHACONAS

SPICED MASHED POTATOES WITH CRISPY PORK BELLY

This traditional tapa comes from Avila in the province of Castilla, the epicentre of Spain. Castilla is a land of history, kingdoms, castles, cathedrals and an outstanding gastronomy. You could say this is a rustic mashed potato dish, spiced up with smoked pimentón and traditionally served with pork crackling.

Serves 4 as a tapa

3 large waxy potatoes (about 500g/1lb 2 oz), peeled and quartered
1 whole head of garlic
½ onion
1 bay leaf
extra virgin olive oil, for frying
300g (10½oz) pork belly, cut into bite-sized chunks
1 tbsp sweet pimentón (sweet smoked paprika)
1 tsp spicy pimentón (hot smoked paprika)
salt and freshly ground black pepper

Put the potatoes, garlic, onion, a pinch of salt and the bay leaf in a pan and cover with water. Bring to the boil and cook over a medium heat for about 25 minutes, or until the potatoes are soft. Drain the potatoes, but reserve a bit of the water, the garlic, onion and bay leaf. Peel the garlic and reserve the pulp.

Heat a drizzle of oil in a frying pan and fry the pork belly pieces with the bay leaf from the potatoes and a bit of salt until crispy (this can take up to 30 minutes). Set the meat aside to rest.

In the same pan, fry the boiled onion, then set aside for later.

Fry the garlic pulp until light golden. Add the sweet and hot pimentón and after 10 seconds add the potatoes, give them a stir and mash them in the pan with a fork. If they get too dry use the reserved cooking water to thin the purée. Season with salt and pepper.

Serve the potatoes with the crispy pork belly and pan-fried onion on top.

ensaladas
SALADS

ENSALADA DE AGUACATE Y CALABAZA ASADA

SALAD OF AVOCADO, LETTUCE, BUTTERNUT SQUASH AND WALNUTS

Serves 6

1 small butternut squash (total weight about 500g/1lb 2oz), cut into slim wedges

a good drizzle of extra virgin olive oil

2 heads little gem lettuce, leaves separated

2 avocados, peeled, stoned and cut into chunks

100g (heaped 1 cup) walnut halves

a few fresh coriander (cilantro) leaves, to garnish

salt

For the vinaigrette
grated zest and juice of 1 lemon
1 tbsp whisky
1 tbsp honey
1 tsp salt
3½ tbsp extra virgin olive oil

Salads don't have to be garnishes, sides or starters. Once a week I always have a big plate of salad as a main course and nothing else. This one will fill you up, big time.

Preheat the oven to 150°C/130°C fan/300°F/gas mark 2 and line a baking sheet with baking paper.

Rub the butternut squash in the olive oil and some salt, spread out on the baking sheet and bake for 30 minutes. Allow to cool.

For the vinaigrette, combine the lemon zest and juice, whisky, honey and salt in a small bowl and whisk for 1 minute. Slowly pour in the olive oil in a thin, steady stream, whisking until the vinaigrette has emulsified.

Place the cooled butternut squash, the lettuce, avocados and two-thirds of the walnut halves into a salad bowl and mix to combine. Roughly chop the rest of the walnuts and sprinkle over the salad. Drizzle with the vinaigrette and garnish with the coriander leaves.

ENSALADA DE CANÓNIGOS, PIMIENTOS Y ATÚN

LAMB'S LETTUCE, ROASTED RED PEPPER AND TUNA SALAD

Serves 6

2 red (bell) peppers or 1 x 250g (9oz) jar roasted red peppers

4 eggs

4 handfuls lamb's lettuce (corn salad)

1 x 200g (7oz) tin/jar green manzanilla olives, or other Spanish variety, drained

2 tbsp sherry vinegar

1 x 170g (6oz) tin tuna in olive oil, Spanish if possible (worth every extra penny), shredded, reserving the oil

a pinch of sea salt

We love tinned foods in Spain, not just because of the flavour but because they are so convenient when you have no time; you will find all sorts of things in tins or jars in the supermarkets. This recipe could be called 'open the tin salad' – so easy, filling and great tasting.

Preheat the oven to 180°C/160°C fan/350°F/gas mark 4 and roast the peppers for 20 minutes, if using fresh peppers. Remove from the oven, cover with a cloth or plastic wrap and leave for 30 minutes. Remove the skins from the softened peppers over a salad bowl to capture all the juices and discard. Alternatively, use jarred ready roasted peppers.

Put the eggs in a pan of cold water and bring to the boil, cooking for about 5 minutes in total. Cool them down by running them under cold water and then peel and cut into halves. They should be firm but not overcooked – there is a fine line we should never cross.

Mix together all the ingredients in the salad bowl, season with the salt and use the olive oil from the tuna as a dressing.

ENSALADA CAMPERA

NEW POTATO, TUNA AND EGG SALAD

Serves 4

4 eggs

400g (14oz, about 3 cups) new potatoes

1 tsp + a pinch salt

2 tomatoes (weighing 250g/9oz in total), cut into wedges

1 red (bell) pepper, chopped into 1cm (⅜in) dice

1 green (bell) pepper, chopped into 1cm (⅜in) dice

½ red onion, thinly sliced

100g (1 cup) green and black pitted olives

1 x 170g (6oz) tin tuna in olive oil

3 tbsp sherry vinegar

5 tbsp extra virgin olive oil

1 tbsp finely chopped flat-leaf parsley

This is one of those salads that is incredibly popular in Spanish households, not just in mine. The name translates literally as 'country salad', so maybe it's this outdoors-y name that makes us cook it for picnics and BBQs.

Place the eggs and potatoes in a pan, add a pinch of salt and cover with cold water. Bring to the boil over a high heat and, after a total of 5 minutes, take out the eggs. Cool them down by running them under cold water and then peel and cut into quarters. The potatoes shouldn't take longer than 20 minutes to cook, but check them after 15 minutes by piercing them with a paring knife. If they feel soft inside, drain and set aside to cool down, then cut in half and place in a big salad bowl.

Add the tomato wedges, diced peppers, sliced red onion and olives to the bowl and mix together with all the ingredients. Open the tin of tuna and use the fishy olive oil from the tin to dress the salad, as well as adding a generous amount of salt, the sherry vinegar and extra virgin olive oil, and give it all a really good stir.

Sprinkle over the finely chopped parsley, arrange the egg quarters over the top and serve.

ENSALADA DE COGOLLOS, CALAMAR Y PIQUILLOS

HOT PAN-FRIED SQUID, LETTUCE AND PIQUILLO PEPPER SALAD

Serves 4 as a tapa

300g (10½oz) fresh squid tubes, cleaned (you can ask your fishmonger to do this for you)

2 garlic cloves, very finely chopped

a few leaves of flat-leaf parsley, very finely chopped

2 tbsp olive oil, plus extra for frying

juice of 1 lemon

1 head little gem lettuce, leaves separated

½ x 220g (7oz) tin/jar piquillo peppers

50g (½ cup) pitted black olives

salt and freshly ground black pepper

At home in wintertime you don't feel like eating as many salads as you do in the summer. This recipe will feel very healthy in the winter months and at the same time it will warm you and fill you up like a main course.

Open the squid tubes and score the inside in a cross-hatch pattern, then cut into small rectangular pieces.

Mix together the chopped garlic and parsley, 2 tablespoons of the olive oil, the lemon juice and some salt and pepper to make a vinaigrette.

Place a large frying pan over a high heat and drizzle with more olive oil. Season the squid and pan-fry for a couple of minutes. Set aside. Add a bit more oil to the pan and cook the lettuce leaves for a few seconds.

Place the piquillo peppers, olives, squid and lettuce leaves on a plate. Drizzle the vinaigrette over the top and enjoy while still warm.

ENSALADILLA RUSA

RUSSIAN TUNA AND POTATO SALAD

Serves 6 as a tapa

4 potatoes (about 500g/1lb 2oz in total), skin on

2 eggs

4 medium carrots, peeled

a handful garden peas

1 x 160g (6oz) tin tuna in brine, drained and shredded

4 small pickled cornichons, finely chopped

about 20 pitted green olives, halved

200g (scant 1 cup) Mayonnaise (see page 27)

salt

This summery dish is the Russian version of the classic potato salad. Although the original recipe contained pheasant and caviar, the Spaniards managed to create a more cost-effective recipe, replacing the meat and other expensive ingredients with tinned tuna, peas or carrots. There are several variations on this salad, which can be prepared ahead and kept in the fridge for two or three days. It is delicious as a starter or as a tapa with toast.

Put the whole potatoes, eggs and carrots in a pan and cover with plenty of cold salted water. Bring to the boil over a high heat and cook for about 45 minutes, or until the potatoes are soft and fully cooked. Remove the eggs from the pan after 8 minutes and the carrots after 20 minutes and run them under cold water to stop them from cooking further.

Fill a small saucepan with water, put over a high heat and bring to the boil. Cook the peas for 2 minutes, drain and run under cold water. Cut the potatoes and carrots into 1–2cm (⅜–¾in) cubes. Peel and grate the eggs, or chop them with a knife.

Put the potatoes, carrots, eggs, shredded tuna, cornichons and peas into a mixing bowl with the olives. Add the mayonnaise and mix all the ingredients until well combined.

COGOLLOS DE TUDELA CON VINAGRETA DE PANCETA
GRILLED LETTUCE WITH SWEET AND SOUR BACON VINAIGRETTE

This is another of my mum's dishes. She has always been famous in our family for her salads – which she brings to all family gatherings. I love the concept of hot salads, particularly in wintertime when you need something to warm you up.

Serves 4 as a starter

½ red onion, sliced

4 tbsp sherry vinegar

50g (2oz) smoked pancetta or bacon, diced

a pinch of sweet pimentón (sweet smoked paprika)

1 tbsp honey

2 heads little gem lettuce, sliced in half lengthways

4 tbsp extra virgin olive oil

a pinch of sea salt

Place the red onion in a small bowl and pour the sherry vinegar over the top. Set aside to marinate.

In a small pan over a high heat, dry-fry the pancetta or bacon until crisp. Sprinkle over the sweet pimentón and then add the honey. After 30 seconds, pour over the sherry vinegar and onions to deglaze the pan. Turn the heat off under the pan and leave to sit.

Heat a separate pan over a high heat until it is as hot as possible. Place the lettuce halves in the pan, cut sides down, and cook for 1 minute, then drizzle with the olive oil and continue to fry for no longer than 1 minute. They will darken quite quickly without losing their raw texture.

Place the cooked lettuces on a serving platter, grilled sides up, and season with a little salt. Pour the hot vinaigrette over the top and enjoy.

ENSALADA DE SANDÍA, TOMATES Y QUESO

WATERMELON, TOMATO, CORIANDER AND GOAT'S CHEESE SALAD

Serves 4

200g (7oz) peeled watermelon, seeded and diced

about 500g (1lb 2oz) yellow or heritage cherry tomatoes, halved

50g (2oz) soft goat cheese

a few sprigs of fresh coriander (cilantro), leaves separated and finely chopped

For the vinaigrette
1 garlic clove, peeled

a good drizzle of balsamic vinegar

½ red onion, thinly sliced

a handful of black olives

a good drizzle of extra virgin olive oil

a pinch of sea salt

Tomatoes are one of my top ingredients yet it is so hard to find good ones in non-sunny countries. Similarly, watermelon is in my top three fruits – so refreshing – and back in Spain they are so delicious. The mix of the two with the salty touch of the cheese makes a terrific salad.

For the vinaigrette, crush the garlic clove with the side of a knife and mix it with the balsamic vinegar in a small bowl. Add the red onion, olives and the oil. Leave to marinate.

Place the watermelon and tomatoes in a bowl. Crumble over the goat cheese and scatter with the coriander.

Drizzle the vinaigrette over the salad, scatter with sea salt and serve.

Easy variation
If you want to add some leaves to this salad, I recommend rocket (arugula).

ENSALADA CALIENTE DE CALAMAR, CHORIZO Y ENDIVIAS

PAN-FRIED SQUID WITH SPICY CHORIZO AND CHICORY SALAD

You have probably noticed how much squid there is in this book. Well, this is a true reflection of how much squid we actually eat in Spain. We love it in all its ways, not just in the ubiquitous deep-fried version. In this unusual salad you will find the saltiness of the pan-fried squid and chorizo combined with the bitterness of the chicory and the acidity of the sherry vinegar is a match made in heaven.

Serves 4 as a tapa

- 4 small or 1 large squid (about 400g/14oz), cleaned (or ask your fishmonger to do this for you)
- 4 tbsp extra virgin olive oil
- 2 heads chicory (endive), leaves separated
- 2 spring onions (scallions), thinly sliced
- 2 tomatoes, cut into wedges
- 1 spicy cooking chorizo (fresh uncooked) sausage, sliced
- 2 tbsp sherry vinegar
- sea salt

Prepare the squid by cutting it into small pieces and scoring the smooth flesh in a cross-hatch pattern.

Heat the oil in a frying pan over a high heat. Add the squid and a pinch of salt and fry the pieces on one side until golden, about 1 minute. Flip the squid and cook the other side (the total cooking time should be no more than 2 minutes).

Meanwhile, mix the chicory, spring onions and tomatoes together in a bowl.

Sauté the chorizo in a frying pan over a medium heat for a couple of minutes, or until cooked. Remove from the heat and swirl the sherry vinegar into the pan.

Add the cooked chorizo and its vinegar, and the cooked squid, to the salad and finish with a drizzle of olive oil and a sprinkling of sea salt.

ESGARRAET VALENCIANO

ROASTED RED PEPPER AND SALT COD SALAD

Valencia is not just about paella. There is a very rich food culture, including this summery dish made with salt cod. Salted, shredded cured cod is easily found in the Jamaican section of any store, but Spanish or Icelandic salt cod is even better if you can find it. 'Esgarraet' in Valencian means 'to shred', which is what we are about to do with this salad.

Serves 6 as a tapa

450–500g (1lb) salt cod

8 large red (bell) peppers

5 tbsp extra virgin olive oil, plus extra for drizzling

2 large garlic cloves, thinly sliced

1 tsp brown sugar

salt

finely chopped flat-leaf parsley, to garnish

Soak the salt cod in cold water for 24 hours, changing the water 3 times during this time. Shred into small pieces using two forks.

Preheat the oven to 220°C/200°C fan/425°F/gas mark 7.

Place the red peppers on a roasting tray and rub all over with the olive oil and some salt. Roast for 25 minutes, turning the peppers halfway through. Remove from the oven and transfer to a bowl of cold water, cover with plastic wrap and leave to rest for at least 30 minutes.

Discard the water from the bowl and use your fingers to peel away and discard the skin from the peppers. Tear the flesh into thick strips and place in a serving bowl or platter with the juices.

Add the sliced garlic, a good drizzle of extra virgin olive oil, the sugar and the shredded salt cod. Garnish with the finely chopped parsley and serve.

Easy tip
The longer this dish has to rest before serving, the more flavour it will develop.

ENSALADA DE FRISÉE Y GRANADA

FRISSÉE LETTUCE, POMEGRANATE AND OLIVE SALAD

I have discovered on my travels that in most countries bitterness is not a taste that is appreciated. In Spain, it is. A short time ago someone told me that most foods which are bitter are very good for the liver as they help to cleanse it and get rid of the bad stuff. Apparently we crave them without noticing. This salad couldn't be any more refreshing.

Serves 4

1 head frisée lettuce, washed and dried
1 x 200g (7oz) tin/jar Spanish pitted black olives, roughly chopped
1 pomegranate
1 tbsp pumpkin seeds

For the dressing
1 tsp sea salt
1 tsp honey
3 tbsp sherry vinegar
150ml (scant ⅔ cup) olive oil

Chop the lettuce into small pieces, discarding the very bitter outer and greener leaves. Place in a salad bowl with the olives.

Cut off the top third of the pomegranate and scoop out the flesh and seeds with a spoon, capturing any juice in a small bowl for the dressing. Tap the scooped chunks over the salad bowl with the back of a spoon to release the seeds; discard the flesh. Squeeze any seeds that don't tap out into the dressing bowl with the juice. You want about 3 tablespoons pomegranate juice.

For the dressing, add the salt, honey and sherry vinegar to the pomegranate juice and whisk together to mix. Slowly pour in the olive oil in a steady stream, whisking constantly until the dressing emulsifies.

Dress the salad and sprinkle the pumpkin seeds over the top to serve.

sopas, legumbres y estofados
SOUPS, PULSES & STEWS

SOPA DE GUISANTES CON JAMÓN

PEA SOUP WITH SERRANO HAM

An amazingly warming, rich and healthy soup, this is made in just 20 minutes from start to finish. Frozen peas are so convenient and I reckon lots of people always have them in their freezer. No excuse not to try this one; I do it myself at home frequently.

Serves 4

4 tbsp extra virgin olive oil
2 slices rustic bread
3 garlic cloves, finely chopped
1 onion, finely chopped
1 bay leaf
50g (2oz) Serrano ham slices, finely chopped, plus 4 extra slices to serve
1 tsp sweet pimentón (sweet smoked paprika)
1 tbsp plain (all-purpose) flour
1 tbsp sherry vinegar
600ml (2½ cups) chicken stock
500g (4 cups) frozen peas
salt and freshly ground black pepper

Pour 1 tablespoon of the oil into a medium pan over a medium heat and fry the bread on both sides. Set aside.

Pour the rest of the oil into the pan, add the garlic, onion, bay leaf and the finely chopped ham and fry for 10 minutes.

Sprinkle over the sweet pimentón and the flour and let it cook for 1 minute, then pour in the sherry vinegar, stirring constantly, and cook for a couple of minutes to make a roux. Increase the temperature to high and continue to stir as you slowly pour in the chicken stock so that the roux dissolves in the stock without forming lumps. Add the frozen peas, season with salt and pepper and leave to boil for 6 minutes.

Top the sliced bread with the rest of the Serrano ham and serve alongside the soup.

Easy tip
You may prefer a smoother soup at the end. If that is the case, blitz to your liking!

SOPA DE MELÓN

CHILLED MELON SOUP

Serves 4

1½ piel de sapo or honeydew melons, peeled, seeded and cut into chunks

2 mint leaves

30g (1oz) Serrano ham, very finely chopped, to serve, optional

a drizzle of single (light) cream, optional

or

3½ tbsp extra virgin olive oil

This is a summer dish that will refresh you in hot weather. It is normally eaten with Serrano ham shavings. However, you can omit it if you're cooking for vegetarians. In Spain, we use a local melon called 'piel de sapo'. Your soup will taste completely different depending on which type of melon you use, which, in my view, is all the fun.

Blend the melon chunks with the mint until you have a melon soup that is completely blended. Chill for at least 30 minutes in the fridge.

Give the chilled soup a good stir to bring it together again and serve, with the finely chopped ham and a drizzle of cream or extra virgin olive oil, if you like.

Easy tip
To crisp up the ham, put it in the microwave on a plate and cook it for 30 seconds.

GAZPACHO DE SANDÍA

CHILLED WATERMELON SOUP

Serves 2

500g (1lb 2oz) watermelon, peeled and chopped

4 tomatoes, chopped

1 red (bell) pepper, chopped

¼ cucumber, chopped

¼ onion, chopped

½ garlic clove, chopped

1 slice of rustic bread, chopped

1 tsp salt

1 tsp ground cumin

3 tbsp sherry vinegar

a drizzle of olive oil

This is a recipe that has been enjoyed by thousands of customers in my restaurants – incredibly tasty, so refreshing and full of goodness. In a nutshell, it is a blended salad. You can keep it in a bottle in your fridge for up to three days.

Place all the ingredients except the olive oil in a blender and begin liquidizing. Add the olive oil, a little at a time, and continue blending until smooth. Check the seasoning and adjust if necessary. Serve over ice.

Easy tip
If you want to serve this as a starter and make it a bit more filling, serve it in a soup bowl with croutons and a drizzle of extra virgin olive oil.

SOUPS, PULSES & STEWS

BACALAO CON LENTEJAS SALTEADAS
COD AND LENTIL STEW

Serves 4

7 tbsp olive oil, plus extra to serve
5 garlic cloves, thinly sliced
½ onion, thinly sliced
2 red chilli peppers, chopped
1 tsp sweet pimentón (sweet smoked paprika)
1 x 400g (14oz) tin cooked lentils, drained
1½ tbsp amontillado sherry
a handful fresh flat-leaf parsley, leaves separated
4 x 200g (7oz) cod loins
salt and freshly ground black pepper

A truly healthy dish, simply cooked with a convenient tin of cooked lentils. Across Castilla pulses are so popular, particularly as part of stews. We should all eat more pulses.

Heat 6 tablespoons of the oil in a pan over a medium heat and cook the garlic, onion and chilli until the onion is light golden. Sprinkle over the sweet pimentón and quickly add the lentils and sherry. Season with salt and pepper, add the parsley leaves, stir to combine and then immediately turn off the heat.

Pour the remaining tablespoon of olive oil into another pan over a medium heat and cook the cod loins, skin-side down, for about 5 minutes depending on the thickness of the loin, before flipping it over to finish cooking on the other side for a minute or so. Season to your liking.

Serve the cod loins with the lentils and a drizzle of olive oil on top.

Easy tip
I use these lentils in so many different recipes – sometimes in a salad or sometimes as above, but with a chicken breast instead of the cod.

CARNE GOBERNADA
BEEF STEW

Serves 4

1 x 700–900g (1½–2lb) shin (foreshank) of beef

4 garlic cloves, roughly chopped

1 tbsp rock salt

olive oil

1 large onion, roughly chopped

1 red (bell) pepper, roughly chopped

1 green (bell) pepper, roughly chopped

1 carrot, roughly chopped

1 leek, roughly chopped

1 tbsp sweet pimentón (sweet smoked paprika)

120ml (½ cup) white wine

1 litre (4⅓ cups) beef stock

sourdough bread or fried potatoes, to serve

This is a very slow-cooked beef stew traditionally made in Asturias, northern Spain, and perfect for cold winter days. It is a simple recipe but it is essential to control the heat to get the flavours and textures right. Nowadays it's rarely found in Spanish restaurants and that's why I wanted to include it here. Who knows, perhaps it will become popular again! I like to prepare it the day before serving, and eat it with sourdough or fried potatoes.

Dice the beef and place it in a bowl with the chopped garlic, rock salt and a splash of olive oil, cover with plastic wrap and leave in the fridge for 24 hours.

The following day, remove the garlic from the meat. Heat 3 tablespoons of olive oil in a large pan over a high heat and fry the beef for a couple of minutes to seal it. Add all the roughly chopped vegetables and cook for about 10 minutes. Once all the vegetables are soft, add the sweet pimentón and mix well before adding the wine. Leave to cook until the liquid has reduced by half.

Add the beef stock, reduce the heat to a simmer and then cover and leave to stew slowly for at least 2 hours, or until the meat is tender. Check from time to time that you do not run out of liquid; you can add water if this happens.

Serve with sourdough bread or fried potatoes.

Easy tip
In Spain we use pressure cookers a lot and they're very helpful for preparing these kinds of dishes. Try it – you could have this stew ready in half the time!

SOUPS, PULSES & STEWS

CAZUELA DE LANGOSTA

LOBSTER AND SAFFRON PASTA STEW

Serves 4

400ml (1¾ cups) fresh fish stock, or 1 fish stock cube dissolved in 400ml (1¾ cups) water

1 tsp saffron threads, ground into a powder

4 tbsp extra virgin olive oil

½ onion, finely chopped

1 dried cayenne pepper (or any other dried red chilli pepper)

1 bay leaf

1 lobster

12 blanched roasted almonds

2 tbsp breadcrumbs

3 garlic cloves

1 salted anchovy

1 tsp tomato purée (paste)

1½ tbsp brandy

1½ tbsp white wine

1 piece (10g/1½oz) dark (bittersweet) chocolate

100g (3½oz) thin 3-minute spaghetti, broken into 3cm (1¼in) pieces

3 sprigs fresh flat-leaf parsley, finely chopped

salt and freshly ground black pepper

This dish is a real showstopper in terms of flavour. After I cooked it in under 8 minutes on national TV, all the guests were asking me, 'How did you make something so good in 8 minutes?' They couldn't believe it. Lobster is not cheap but for a special occasion, give this recipe a go.

Bring the fish stock to the boil in a large pan over a high heat and add the saffron.

Meanwhile, pour the olive oil into a frying pan over a high heat and add the onion, cayenne pepper and bay leaf. Let it sizzle for a couple of minutes.

To prepare the lobster, cut the head in half lengthways and separate the head from the tail. Cut the tail horizontally into 2cm (¾in) (30g/1oz) pieces. Twist off the claws but leave them whole. Add all the pieces to the pan.

Tip the almonds, breadcrumbs, garlic, anchovy and tomato purée into a small food processor and blend to a paste. Add to the pan.

Stir the pan for 1 minute and then flambé with the brandy and white wine. To do this, slowly tilt the pan towards the flame until the brandy catches, or light with a match. Let the flames flare up then die down and then add the boiling saffron-infused fish stock, the chocolate and pasta. Season with salt and pepper and leave to boil for 3 minutes until the pasta is al dente and the lobster is perfectly cooked. Garnish with the parsley and serve.

SOUPS, PULSES & STEWS

POTAJE CANARIO

CANARY ISLAND MEAT AND VEGETABLE STEW

Serves 6

2 garlic cloves, peeled

½ bunch fresh parsley

extra virgin olive oil

4 floury potatoes

1 carrot

1 onion

150g (5½oz) marrow or courgette (zucchini)

200g (7oz) squash, any kind

300g (10½oz) pork ribs (ask your butcher to cut them into medium-sized pieces)

2 corn cobs, each cut into 3 pieces

1 tsp smoked pimentón (sweet smoked paprika)

450ml (1¾ cups) meat or vegetable stock

100g (3½oz) flat green beans or runner beans

1 x 400g (14oz) tin chickpeas (garbanzo beans), drained and rinsed

100g (3½oz) spring greens, roughly chopped

salt

As its name suggests, this stew is typical of the Canary Islands. Corn is well used there along with other more tropical produce (like mangoes, bananas, custard apples, pineapples) because of their climate and their South American heritage; historically, most journeys to the Americas had to stop in the Islands as it was the first pit stop after crossing the Atlantic and vice versa.

Use a pestle and mortar to grind the garlic, parsley, a drizzle of olive oil and pinch of salt to make a paste and set aside.

Peel and roughly dice 1 of the potatoes, the carrot, onion, marrow or courgette and squash. Place all of these vegetables into a large stockpot together with the ribs, corn, the garlic paste and the pimentón. Add the stock, a drizzle of olive oil and enough water to cover all the ingredients and give it a good stir. Heat over a high heat and bring to the boil, then reduce the heat to medium-low and simmer for about 30 minutes, stirring from time to time. The potato will slowly break up and thicken the stew.

Meanwhile, peel the rest of the potatoes and dice them into 1.5cm (½in) cubes. Remove the strings from the beans and cut each one into 4 pieces. Add to the pan with the chickpeas and spring greens and cook over a medium heat for a further 15 minutes. Turn off the heat, cover and leave to rest for another 15 minutes before serving.

RAGÚ DE CARRILLERAS CON PASTA

STEWED PIG CHEEKS WITH PASTA

Pasta has been used in Spanish cooking for centuries due to the close links the east coast of Spain and the Balearic Islands had with Italy's west coast, Corsica and Sardinia. From Roman times we have always had a great cultural and trading relationship, and good things, as good habits, spread fast. This pasta stew is rich and intense with so many layers of flavour that blend very well with the plain pasta.

Serves 4

500g (1lb 2oz) pig (pork) cheeks, trimmed
5 tbsp extra virgin olive oil
½ large onion, finely chopped
½ celery stick, finely chopped
4 garlic cloves, finely chopped
1 large carrot, finely chopped
3 sprigs fresh thyme
1 bay leaf
2 tomatoes, quartered
150ml (scant ⅔ cup) red wine
2 litres (2 quarts) chicken stock
300g (10½oz) pasta shells
salt and freshly ground black pepper

Lightly season the pig cheeks with salt and pepper. Heat the olive oil in a large heavy-based pan over a high heat and seal the cheeks on both sides. Remove the meat and set aside.

Add the onion, celery, garlic and carrot to the pan, adding more oil if necessary. Fry until dark golden and caramelized, about 8–10 minutes. Add the thyme, bay leaf and tomatoes and continue to cook for 5 minutes, then add the pig cheeks and red wine. Cook for 2 minutes to reduce the liquid, then pour in the stock, reduce the heat to medium and cook for 30 minutes. Reduce the heat again and leave to simmer for at least 2 hours, or longer, until the meat is tender.

Remove the pig cheeks from the pan and shred using a masher or fork. Return the shredded meat to the pan and simmer for a further 5 minutes. You will need enough liquid in the pan to cook the pasta with enough left for sauce. Add more water if necessary and add the pasta to the pan. Give it a good stir and cook over a low heat according to the packet instructions, until the pasta is al dente. The starch released by the pasta should thicken the stew, giving it a great body and consistency. If it looks too dry, add more water halfway through cooking the pasta.

POTAJE MONTAÑÉS

CHORIZO, GREENS AND BEAN STEW

I had only tried this dish once in my life before I cooked it for this book. I had it in the city of Santander with all my friends at the wedding of our dear friend Pablo. It was so good I have never forgotten about it. Note that you will need to soak the dried butter (lima) beans overnight before you start cooking.

Serves 6

350g (2 cups) dried butter (lima) beans

500g (1lb 2oz) pork belly, cut into 3cm (1¼in) chunks

3 smoked cooking chorizo (fresh uncooked) sausages (about 100g/3½oz each)

3 black puddings (about 100g/3½oz each)

2 bay leaves

4 tbsp olive oil

4 garlic cloves, thinly sliced

50g (2oz) Serrano ham, diced

1 tbsp plain (all-purpose) flour

1 tsp sweet pimentón (sweet smoked paprika)

1 head of spring greens (or any green cabbage), roughly chopped

Soak the dried beans in cold water overnight.

The next day, put the soaked and drained beans, pork belly, chorizo sausages, black puddings and bay leaves in a large saucepan and pour in about 3 litres (3 quarts) cold water.

Bring to the boil over a high heat then cook at a rolling simmer for 1 hour, skimming the froth that appears on the surface with the help of a ladle.

Pour the olive oil into a frying pan over a low heat and fry the garlic and Serrano ham for 5 minutes without getting any colour on them. Sprinkle the flour and pimentón into the pan and stir for a couple of minutes to form a roux.

Take a ladleful of liquid from the large saucepan and add it to the roux. Stir until combined and add another ladleful if necessary. Pour the contents of the frying pan into the large pan and stir. The roux will eventually make the stew a little thicker and have a better texture, instead of seeming like a soup.

Simmer for 2½–3 hours in total until the beans are soft, and add the spring greens 30 minutes before the end of the cooking time.

Serve in soup bowls, making sure everyone has equal portions of the different meats.

FABES CON ALMEJAS
CLAM AND BEAN STEW

This is another splendid example of a brilliant bean stew. Look for good-quality clams and pamper the beans – it is worth it.

Serves 6

500g (3 cups) dried butter (lima) beans
1 onion, cut in half
1 bay leaf
a pinch of saffron threads
500g (1lb 2oz) clams, cleaned and any open or damaged shells discarded
25g (1½ tbsp) butter
1 tbsp extra virgin olive oil
a bunch of spring onions (scallions), chopped
4 garlic cloves, finely chopped
1 tbsp plain (all-purpose) flour
250ml (1 generous cup) white wine
3 tbsp finely chopped parsley
salt

Soak the dried beans in cold water overnight.

The next day, put the soaked and drained beans in a heavy-based saucepan with the onion and bay leaf. Pour in about 3 litres (3 quarts) cold water but do not add salt.

Bring to the boil over a high heat, skimming the froth that appears on the surface with the help of a ladle. Then, set the heat to low and simmer for at least 3 hours, until the beans are soft. Add the saffron after 1 hour and skim the surface from time to time. Reserve the cooking liquor.

Put the clams in a large bowl or in the sink, cover with cold salty water and leave for 1 hour, moving them around with your hand from time to time. This will help the clams to open and release any sand.

Melt the butter in a frying pan with the olive oil over a medium heat. Add the spring onions and cook until soft, then add the garlic and, after a minute, the flour. Stir it constantly for 2 minutes to toast the flour, then add the white wine. Give it a good last stir to prevent lumps from forming. Add the clams along with the parsley, the beans and a litre of the reserved cooking liquor.

Once the clams are open, mix everything together well and season to taste.

Easy swap
You can buy ready-cooked beans in a jar and you will have the same results in just 15 minutes.

paella y arroces
PAELLA & RICE

PAELLA DE MARISCO
SEAFOOD PAELLA

Serves 5

500g (1lb 2oz) fresh squid, inner parts removed but kept (you can ask your fishmonger to do this for you)

3½ tbsp extra virgin olive oil

1 tbsp rock or sea salt, plus extra for seasoning

1 red romano or bell pepper, cut into thick strips

200g (7oz) flat green or runner beans, chopped (this is optional, but I like it)

6 garlic cloves, finely chopped

1 tsp sweet pimentón (sweet smoked paprika)

2 tomatoes (weighing about 300g/10½oz in total), grated

400g (heaped 2 cups) paella rice, such as Bomba, Senia or Bahia

500g (1lb 2oz) prawns (shrimp) or langoustines, or a mixture, a few reserved whole, otherwise heads and shells removed

10 mussels and/or clams, cleaned and any open or damaged shells discarded

How good this book is comes down to how good this recipe tastes. If you follow it, my friends and family say it is one of the very best paellas they have tasted. The intensity of flavour in the stock you make will be the most important thing, as well as how wide your paella pan is. Believe it or not, it makes all the difference. On a conventional hob at home, to achieve perfection you cannot cook a really good paella for more than three people. The caramelization of the ingredients and how the rice sears over the wide surface adds points to the flavour and end result. Having said all these things to satisfy the purists, for us home cooks (I include myself), if you cook it for more than three it still tastes amazing. I do it all the time.

To clean the squid at home, remove the inner parts with your fingers, cutting the inner core just above the tentacles. Don't discard any of these ugly parts as they will make a rich stock.

First make the stock (see next page for ingredients). Heat a good drizzle of extra virgin olive oil in a casserole dish over the highest heat. Add the heads and shells of the prawns and langoustines and brown them for 2 minutes. Add the reserved inner parts of the squid, the carrot, onion, celery, leek, garlic halves, black peppercorns and bay leaf and let caramelize until the vegetables are a dark golden colour, then add the tomato.

Cook for 2 minutes and then flambé with the brandy followed by the white wine. To do this, pour the alcohol into the dish and light with a match, keeping your head and hair well back. Let the flames flare up then die down. Continue to cook until the alcohol burns off and reduces down until completely evaporated, then add 3 litres (3 quarts) water and the fish bones or stock cubes.

Recipe and ingredients continue overleaf

For the shellfish stock
extra virgin olive oil, for frying
heads and shells of 500g (1lb 2oz) prawns and langoustines (see previous page)
the inner parts of the fresh squid (see previous page), ink included
1 carrot, roughly chopped
1 onion, roughly chopped
1 celery stick, roughly chopped
1 small leek, roughly chopped
1 head of garlic, halved
3 black peppercorns
1 bay leaf
1 tomato, roughly chopped
3½ tbsp brandy
120ml (½ cup) white wine
3 white fish carcasses or 1 head of cod or monkfish, or 2 fish stock cubes
1g (2 tsp) saffron threads

Simmer the stock for no longer than 45 minutes, using a hand blender to blitz it after 30 minutes (yes, shells and bones included) to extract as much flavour as possible out of every ingredient. After 45 minutes, pass through a very fine sieve into another pot. You should have about 2 litres (2 quarts) of intense, flavoursome shellfish stock. Add the saffron and reduce the heat to a simmer until needed.

Roughly chop the squid tube, wings and tentacles.

Place your paella or wide frying pan over the highest heat with the olive oil, chopped squid and salt. Let the water from the squid evaporate before adding the red pepper and green beans (if using), stirring constantly so that all the ingredients brown nicely. Add the garlic and stir for 1 minute before adding the sweet pimentón. Stir again and cook for 30 seconds, then add the tomatoes. If the garlic or pimentón start to burn, add the tomatoes a little earlier. Add the rice and stir for 2 minutes to sear the rice and give a slightly crispier bite to the end dish. It will also mean the rice loses less starch, making the grain feel looser. Pour over the hot stock and give everything a good stir, scraping the bottom of the pan to ensure all the caramelization is incorporated into the stock. Taste the seasoning at this point – it should taste slightly over salted (don't worry: the rice will absorb it and balance it all out). Adjust if necessary.

The rice should be ready in about 18 minutes. Put your timer on and remember this will be the last time you stir the rice. Now it is time to let it cook on its own, we will only need to manage the heat. Let it simmer over the highest heat for 10 minutes, or until the liquid has reduced down to almost level with the rice, then reduce the heat to low and scatter the prawns, langoustines, mussels and/or clams over the top of the rice. Top with the reserved whole prawns. Season them lightly. They will steam gently above the paella.

Leave to cook for the remaining 8 minutes, until the liquid is gone and you can hear that the rice in the bottom of the pan is starting to fry. Put your ear close to the pan without burning your hair and let the paella talk to you. It should say, 'I am getting crispier on the bottom, this is good but don't let me burn, please.'

After 5 minutes of resting time you should dig in. As the Spanish say, 'Rice doesn't wait for anyone; everyone should wait at the table for the rice to come.'

ARROZ MELOSO DE GAMBAS Y ALCACHOFAS

CREAMY RICE WITH PRAWNS AND ARTICHOKES

Serves 5

500g (1lb 2oz) fresh squid, cleaned (you can ask your fishmonger to do this for you)

10 baby artichokes, stalks trimmed and outer leaves removed

3½ tbsp extra virgin olive oil

1 tbsp rock or sea salt

1 onion, roughly chopped

6 garlic cloves, finely chopped

1 tsp sweet pimentón (sweet smoked paprika)

2 tomatoes (weighing about 300g/10½oz in total), grated

1g (2 tsp) saffron threads

2 litres (2 quarts) shellfish stock (see pages 152–154)

400g (heaped 2 cups) Spanish paella rice, such as Bomba, Bahia or Senia

500g (1lb 2oz) prawns (shrimp), heads and shells removed

This rice dish is a megahit in my home. The artichokes give a beautiful liquorice flavour, which I love. People don't cook much with artichokes but I grew up with them. My mum used to just boil them whole and serve them with olive oil to dip in; it felt like a treat back then so I am a big fan. Now my wife and kids are addicted to them, so I have become an artichoke peeling machine, when they are in season!

Roughly chop the squid tube, wings and tentacles.

Cut the artichoke hearts into quarters and scrape away any of the furry choke with a teaspoon. (If you do this step in advance, squeeze over some lemon juice and keep them in cold water to stop them going dark and oxidizing.)

Place a large wide pan (or a big heatproof terracotta one if you have one) over a high heat and add the olive oil, squid and salt. Allow the squid to release its liquid and let it evaporate before adding the onion and artichoke, stirring constantly so that everything browns nicely.

Add the garlic and stir for 1 minute before adding the sweet pimentón. Stir again and cook for 30 seconds, then add the grated tomatoes. If the garlic or pimentón start to burn, add the tomatoes a little earlier. Add the saffron and stock and bring to the boil. Taste and adjust the salt if necessary; it should taste too salty at this stage as it will balance out once the rice is cooked.

Add the rice and cook for 5 minutes over the high heat, then reduce to low and continue to cook for 15 minutes, stirring every now and then. Add the prawn tails just 5 minutes before the rice is ready. The rice should have released a lot of starch with the stirring, making the texture thick and dense, like a risotto.

Recipe pictured overleaf.

ARROZ MELOSO DE SETAS
SOUPY RICE WITH MUSHROOMS AND COD

Serves 5

200g (7oz) salt cod

2 litres (2 quarts) vegetable or beef stock

1 tsp saffron threads

3½ tbsp olive oil

1 tsp salt

1 onion, finely chopped

½ red (bell) pepper, roughly chopped

300g (4½ cups) wild mushrooms or a mix of shiitake and oyster, chopped or torn

5 garlic cloves, finely chopped

1 tsp sweet pimentón (sweet smoked paprika)

1 tomato (about 150g/5½oz), grated

350g (heaped 1¾ cups) paella rice, such as Bomba

This is a creamy paella that is cooked very differently to a dry paella like the Paella de Marisco (see pages 152–154) and Arroz del Senyoret (see pages 160–161) where you don't stir the rice so that it doesn't release any starch. Here is the opposite: you want to stir frequently so that the starch gives a lovely creamy texture to the dish. I like to cook the rice until al dente as, by the time you plate it, sit down at the table and start eating, your rice should be just right. The end result for this dish will rely heavily on the quality and flavour that your chosen mushrooms give the stock, which will end up being absorbed by the rice.

Soak the salt cod in cold water for 24 hours, changing the water 3 times during this time. Shred it into small pieces.

When you are ready to start cooking, bring the stock to the boil in a large pan and add the saffron to infuse. Turn off the heat.

Heat the oil in a large frying pan over a medium heat and add the salt, onion and red pepper. Cook for 5 minutes, then add the mushrooms and cook for 10 minutes. Add the garlic and cook for 1 minute before adding the sweet pimentón and, after 20 seconds, the grated tomato. Cook for another 3 minutes, then add the saffron-infused stock. Bring to the boil and add the rice. Give it a good stir and cook over a high heat for 10 minutes, stirring occasionally.

After 10 minutes, reduce the heat to low and add the shredded salted cod, then cook for 8 more minutes, stirring constantly, until the rice is al dente. Serve and eat right away.

ARROZ DEL SENYORET

LORD'S PAELLA, WITH SHELLFISH BUT NO SHELLS

Serves 4

100ml (scant ½ cup) olive oil

1 tbsp salt

2 fresh squid (600g/1lb 5oz total), cleaned (ask your fishmonger to do this) and chopped

½ small onion, very finely chopped

5 garlic cloves, finely chopped

1 tsp sweet pimentón (sweet smoked paprika)

1 tomato (weighing 150g/5½oz in total), grated

350g (heaped 1¾ cups) Spanish paella rice, such as Bomba

20 whole king prawns (jumbo shrimp) or 20 langoustines, heads and shells removed

salt

For the shellfish stock

heads and shells of 20 prawns (see above)

a drizzle of olive oil

1 leek, thinly sliced

1 celery stick, thinly sliced

1 carrot, thinly sliced

1 head of garlic, cloves separated and finely chopped

1½ tbsp brandy

1½ tbsp white wine

3 litres (3 quarts) fish stock

1 salted anchovy or 1 tsp dried Japanese Bonito flakes or 1 tsp Thai shrimp paste

6 black peppercorns

1 bay leaf

1g (2 tsp) saffron threads, toasted (see Easy tips, opposite)

This is a seafood paella for people who don't fancy getting their hands dirty peeling shellfish while they eat. 'Senyoret' means 'lord' in the Valencian dialect and, back in the day, the lords wanted their food prepared and neat. This recipe relies heavily on the flavour of your fish stock. Ingredients in the Spanish Levante are of the highest quality and full of flavour, whether it is an onion or the fish they make the stock with. These ingredients are incomparable to the ones you find elsewhere sadly, but I have a solution. Whether you buy it or make it from scratch, you will need to give it extra flavour by adding more ingredients before you allow your rice to drink it. This is fundamental to any good rice dish or paella.

I believe that the only way to achieve the flavour that a master arrocero in Valencia will get into his paella is by making a shellfish stock with a previously made fish stock. I know it feels like you're doubling up but, seriously, it allows you to get good intensity and a depth that you will not achieve unless you do this.

For the stock, place the prawn heads and shells in a pan over a high heat with some olive oil. Add the leek, celery, carrot and garlic and cook until golden brown and there is an intense toasted shellfish aroma coming out of the pan.

Flambé with the brandy and wine. To do this, pour the alcohol into the pan and light with a match, keeping your head back. Let the flames flare up then die down, then immediately add the fish stock followed by the anchovy, peppercorns and bay. Simmer for 45 minutes.

Blend the stock to extract as much flavour as possible, then pass through a fine sieve. Pour into a pan over a low heat, add the saffron and simmer for at least 15 minutes.

Meanwhile, prepare the paella. Put the oil and salt into a paella pan or large wide pan over a high heat and then add the squid. When it starts to pop a little bit, lower the heat to medium and add the onion. Fry for 5 minutes before adding the garlic. Continue to fry for about 1 minute, stirring constantly, then add the sweet pimentón and 20 seconds later the tomato. Fry it all together, stirring constantly, for about 4–5 minutes, or until the tomato has reduced down. Scrape the bottom of the pan while the tomato is cooking to release all the sticky bits.

Increase the temperature to its highest setting and add the rice. Give it a good stir to coat it in the sofrito and sear for 2 minutes. Pour in the boiling stock, give it a good stir and boil for 10 minutes. Do not stir the rice again or you will ruin the texture of your paella. After 10 minutes lower the heat to medium and check the seasoning for salt.

Roughly chop the prawn tails and scatter them over the pan, shaking the pan a couple of times to distribute them. Reduce the heat to low and cook for 8 minutes, or until the rice is cooked. Ideally a layer of toasted rice will form on the base of the pan, which unfortunately you cannot see but you can judge by the sound and smell – it should sound like it is crisping up and the smell should be toasty. Leave to rest for 5 minutes, then serve.

Easy tips
You can add mussel meat or other shellfish to this rice, as long as it's cleaned from the shells.

Saffron is the most expensive spice in the world and it's grown in just a few countries. Spanish saffron is regarded as the best and most expensive of all, partly because it is toasted and given an extra layer of flavour. As a result it loses weight, so it's even more precious, gram for gram. If your saffron is not Spanish I recommend you toast it before you use it. Wrap it in foil and hold it with a pair of tongs over an open flame for just 10 seconds, flipping the envelope every other second so that the heat is indirect and even and the saffron doesn't burn. It is extremely fine and delicate.

Recipe pictured overleaf.

PAELLA & RICE

ARROZ AL HORNO

BAKED RICE WITH PORK RIBS AND SAUSAGE

Serves 4

- 750ml (3¼ cups) chicken, pork or beef stock
- 1g (2 tsp) saffron threads
- olive oil
- 1 tomato or 2 cherry tomatoes, halved
- 1 head of garlic, skin on, halved horizontally
- 300g (10½oz) pork ribs or smoked pancetta, cut into small pieces
- 1 small potato, cut into 1–2cm (⅜–¾in) cubes
- 2 whole morcilla (Spanish blood puddings), preferably made with onion
- 4 chipolata sausages or cooking chorizo (fresh uncooked) sausages, cut into small pieces
- 1 tsp sweet pimentón (sweet smoked paprika)
- 1 bay leaf
- 1 tomato, grated
- 350g (heaped 1¾ cups) paella rice
- 150g (heaped 1 cup) tinned chickpeas (garbanzo beans), drained
- salt

This dish is even more popular in Valencia than paella and all my friends from the Mediterranean side of Spain say that it's Granny's star dish for family gatherings – it is traditionally cooked with all the leftover stock and meats from our famous hot pot known as cocido. It is worth using a terracotta pot to cook the entire recipe as it captures all the flavours from beginning to end, but you can also use a pan or roasting tray.

Preheat the oven to 200°C/180°C fan/400°F/gas mark 6.

Bring the stock to the boil in a saucepan. Add the saffron and let it simmer while you prepare the rest of the ingredients.

Place a casserole dish, roasting tray or ovenproof frying pan over a medium heat and heat some olive oil. Fry the tomato and garlic halves until golden and set aside.

Add the ribs, potato cubes and all the sausages to the dish and cook for 15 minutes, or until golden and roasted. Add the sweet pimentón, bay leaf, the grated tomato and salt to season, and fry carefully while stirring for 3–4 minutes. Add the rice and give all the ingredients a good stir. Cook over a medium heat for a further 2 minutes.

Pour the boiling stock into the dish along with the chickpeas and mix well, spreading the rice and meat around the whole dish. Place the garlic head and tomatoes on the top. Cook over the highest heat for 10 minutes and then transfer to the oven for a further 10 minutes.

Once the rice is cooked, leave it to rest for 3–4 minutes before serving in the centre of the table.

postres y dulces
DESSERTS & SWEET TREATS

PIÑA ESTOFADA CON RON Y CREMA DE COCO

POACHED CARAMELIZED PINEAPPLE IN RUM WITH COCONUT CREAM

This is a recipe I learned from my years with the chef Ferran Adrià. It was a very refined dish, as you would expect, served during the summer in a Martini glass with all sorts of foams and innovative touches. This is my stripped-back version, full of flavour and very simple to make.

Serves 3

3 tbsp caster (granulated) sugar, plus 1 tsp
200g (1½ cups) cubed pineapple
1½ tbsp dark rum
50g (¼ cup) coconut cream
100ml (scant ½ cup) double (heavy) cream
1 tsp muscovado sugar

Place a pan over a high heat and sprinkle over the 3 tablespoons of sugar. Cook until caramelized and dark, about 4 minutes, then add the pineapple cubes and sauté. Add 100ml (scant ½ cup) water and the rum to the pan and let simmer over a low heat for about 5 minutes. Chill.

In a separate bowl whip the coconut cream, the teaspoon of sugar and the double cream. Pour a little of the caramelized pineapple into a cocktail glass and top with the coconut whipped cream. Sprinkle with muscovado sugar to finish off.

FRESAS AL BRANDY Y CREMA DE QUESO

STRAWBERRIES POACHED IN BRANDY WITH CHEESE CREAM

I love berries, and strawberries are my favourites. I particularly like them with whipped cream. In this recipe, the strawberries have been lightly cooked and the whipped cream has a surprise addition. Together, they are such a treat.

Serves 4

300g (3 cups) strawberries

5 tbsp caster (granulated) sugar

1½ tbsp brandy

grated zest of 1 lime

For the cheese cream

400ml (1¾ cups) double (heavy) cream

1 vanilla pod, split open lengthways and seeds scraped

50g (¼ cup) caster (granulated) sugar

40g (⅓ cup) goat cheese

For the cheese cream, place a small pan over a low heat and add the cream, vanilla pod and seeds, sugar and goat cheese. Bring just to the boil and then take off the heat and blend to a smooth cream. Set aside to cool.

Place the strawberries, 3 tablespoons of the sugar and the brandy in a small pan over a minimum heat. Cover and cook for 5 minutes, or until the sugar dissolves. Don't let it boil. Set aside to cool.

Mix the lime zest with the remaining 2 tablespoons of sugar and spread out on a plate. Leave in a warm place to dry out.

Once the cheese cream has cooled down, use a whisk to whip it to the consistency of whipped cream.

Serve the poached strawberries topped with the cheese cream and sprinkled with the lime sugar.

HIGOS CON TETILLA ASADOS
BAKED FIGS WITH TETILLA CHEESE

Tetilla is a mild and creamy Spanish cheese that gets its name from its breast-like appearance ('tetilla' means 'breast'). I use it in this recipe because melted tetilla is one of the most satisfying flavours, and because we all need a treat from time to time. Don't forget, food feeds your soul!

Serves 4

8 figs
1 cinnamon stick
200g (7oz) tetilla cheese (or any soft cow's milk cheese)
100g (½ cup) soft brown sugar
1½ tbsp sweet sherry wine, preferably Pedro Ximénez
a knob of butter
bread sticks, to serve

Preheat the oven to 180°C/160°C fan/350°F/gas mark 4.

Slice the figs in half and place them in a roasting tray with the cinnamon stick. Break the cheese into pieces and spread it over the figs. Sprinkle with the sugar and the sweet sherry. Finish with a knob of butter and bake for 15–20 minutes.

Have some bread sticks to hand and enjoy this simple but very serious treat.

Easy tip
For a really pretty dish, cut a cross in the top of each fig and open them out like flowers before cooking.

Recipe pictured overleaf.

DESSERTS & SWEET TREATS

CREMOSO DE CHOCOLATE

CHOCOLATE GANACHE WITH OLIVE OIL AND SALT

Serves 2

5 gelatine leaves

100ml (scant ½ cup) double (heavy) cream

100ml (scant ½ cup) milk

180g (1 cup) chopped dark (bittersweet) chocolate (70% cocoa solids)

grated zest of ¼ orange

a drizzle of extra virgin olive oil

a pinch of sea salt

This a straightforward chocolate ganache with two very distinctive Spanish twists: olive oil and orange. It can also be used as a filling in a blind-baked pastry case, or for making good truffles.

Soak the gelatine leaves in cold water for at least 10 minutes, then drain, squeezing out all the excess water.

Bring the cream and milk almost to boiling point in a small pan over a medium heat. Take off the heat and add the chopped chocolate, orange zest and gelatine leaves and stir with a spatula or whisk or blend until completely dissolved. Chill in the fridge for 4 hours, or until completely set.

Serve in little pots, and dress with a drizzle of extra virgin olive oil and a pinch of salt. You could also crumble some biscuits to eat it with or even serve it with strawberries.

FRUTAS SECAS AL JEREZ CON CREMA DE MANCHEGO

DRIED FRUITS STEWED IN SHERRY WITH A MANCHEGO CHEESE GANACHE

Serves 6

150g (¾ cup) caster (granulated) sugar

500ml (2 cups) Pedro Ximénez sweet sherry

200g (1½ cups) pitted dates

200g (1½ cups) currants

200g (1½ cups) pitted prunes

400ml (1¾ cups) double (heavy) cream

200g (7oz) Manchego cheese, chopped

100g (½ cup) cream cheese

a handful of pistachios, chopped

In Spain we grow a lot of vegetables and fruits. We supply a good proportion of the whole of Europe's fruit and veg. In the old days exporting was not as easy as it is now and we had to make sure nothing went to waste. A lot of the dried fruits in Spain are made with summer fruits that after the sun-drying process are then enjoyed in winter, particularly at Christmas. This recipe brings them back to life and the salty cheese ganache makes a good balance with the sweetness of the stewed fruits.

Heat a small pan over a medium heat and sprinkle over 100g (½ cup) of the sugar. Add the wine and all the fruit and simmer gently for 1 hour. The fruit will absorb the richness of the wine and soften.

In a separate pan bring the cream, cheeses and the rest of the sugar just to boiling point, stirring constantly with a whisk, and then take off the heat. Blend until smooth and then put back over the heat, whisking constantly until the mixture comes back to the boil. Blend again until very smooth. Chill in the fridge until cold and then whip with a whisk until the mixture acquires the texture of whipped cream.

Serve the fruit with a little of the sherry syrup and a spoonful of the Manchego cheese ganache on top. Sprinkle with a few chopped pistachios and serve.

ENSAÏMADA MALLORQUINA
ROLLED FLAKY PASTRY

This is one of the most iconic pastries in Spain. It has earned such a renowned status because it is delicious, not just in flavour but in texture, too. The secret is in the way the pastry is made. By rolling it over itself, you achieve really thin layers once it's baked (like a croissant) and it's a treat to dig into.

Makes 4

7g (scant 1 tsp) dried yeast
200g (1 cup) caster (superfine) sugar
2 medium eggs
600g (4¼ cups) very strong flour
a pinch of salt
vegetable oil, for greasing
100g (scant ½ cup) lard
3 tbsp icing (confectioners') sugar

Optional fillings
50g (2oz) Sobrasada de Mallorca (see page 76) mixed with 50g (scant ¼ cup) lard
or
200ml (scant 1 cup) whipped cream or crème pâtissière

Pour 230ml (1 cup) water into a bowl and add the dried yeast. Allow to dilute and then add the caster sugar, eggs, flour and salt. Mix together to form a dough and then knead for a good 15 minutes, until the dough is so elastic you can almost see through it if stretched. Set aside to rest for 30 minutes, then cut into 4 equal pieces and leave to rest for another 30 minutes.

Grease the work surface and a rolling pin with vegetable oil. Flatten one of the dough portions against the worktop with the palm of your hand and roll it out to a very thin rectangle about 20 x 60cm (8 x 24in). Let rest for 2 minutes while you spread a quarter of the lard over it with your fingers. Now, grab a corner of the flattened dough and stretch it out as far as it will go without breaking and repeat every 10cm (4in) or so around the dough in every direction until you have a rectangle about 50 x 70cm (20 x 28in).

Cut a 5cm (2in) strip from one of the long sides of the rectangle and place it over the end of the perpendicular side of the rectangle (this is what we call the heart of the ensaïmada). Since this style of dough, like pizza dough, is always slightly thicker around the edges, it helps to have an extra layer of dough in the very heart of the pastry to provide some extra thickness. Additionally, when it bakes, the heart remains doughy and moist – delicious! Wrap a thin layer of dough over the heart and keep rolling it over itself until you have a long pastry snake. Repeat with the remaining portions of dough.

Grab the first roll of pastry you made and stretch it until it is over a metre (40in) long. Then roll it up in a spiral, leaving 1cm (½in) between each spiral. Flatten a little and transfer to a baking sheet lined with baking paper. Repeat with the remaining pastries. Leave in a humid, fresh (14°C/57°F) and enclosed environment for no more than 12 hours. You will know it is ready when the pastry coils have risen and expanded enough to stick together.

When you are ready to start baking, preheat the oven to 200°C/180°C fan/400°F/gas mark 6. Put the baking sheet in the top third of the oven and immediately lower the temperature to 180°C/160°C fan/350°F/gas mark 4. Bake the pastries for about 15 minutes with heat top and bottom and the fan running, until the pastries are a dark golden colour. Cool on a wire rack and then dust with a generous amount of icing sugar.

If you want to fill your pastry with Sobrasada de Mallorca, use the Sobrasada-lard paste in the same way we used the lard in the main recipe method. It gives a fantastic savoury result.

To fill your ensaïmada with whipped cream or crème pâtissière, cut open the baked pastry, spread it with the cream, sprinkle with sugar and caramelize with a blow torch before closing.

Easy tip
To achieve the right conditions to prove the pastries I wet 2 pieces of paper towels, cut them into pieces, roll into balls and place around the pastries and in the corners of the baking sheet. I place a deep roasting tray upside-down over the pastries, wrap them in plastic wrap and leave somewhere fresh.

Recipe pictured overleaf.

DESSERTS & SWEET TREATS

TURRÓN DE ALMENDRA

ROASTED ALMOND NOUGAT

Let's talk about Christmas. In Spain we have some of the same traditions as in the UK and US, but different ingredients: Spanish Christmas songs, food and, of course, sweets. In all homes across Spain, we have turrón to finish a copious dinner. You could say that turrón is the Spanish fruit cake.

Makes 1 bar

- 300g (2⅓ cups) good-quality raw almonds, ideally Spanish, such as Marcona, skinless
- 1 egg white
- 200g (¾ cup) honey
- 100g (½ cup) caster (superfine) sugar
- ½ tsp ground cinnamon

Preheat the oven to 200°C/180°C fan/400°F/gas mark 6.

Spread the raw almonds over a roasting tray and roast them for 3–4 minutes, or until lightly golden. Set aside to cool, then crush in a food processor. Be careful not to pulverize the almonds as they will release juices and oils that are needed for a good consistency later on.

Whisk the egg white in a clean, grease-free bowl until it is an opaque white foam. This will take a few minutes with an electric whisk or in a mixer.

Put the honey, sugar and cinnamon into a heavy-based pan over a low-medium heat and stir with a wooden spoon or spatula until the sugar has melted with the honey. Remove from the heat and add the egg foam, little by little, whisking and mixing continuously. Place the pan back over a low heat and add the crushed almonds, a little at a time, still stirring and mixing with a wooden spoon or a spatula as the mixture thickens, for no longer than 5 minutes.

If your mixture splits for some reason, you can blend this mix in the food processor again for 30 seconds and it will come back together.

Pour the mixture into a rectangular silicone mould or a baking tin (about 25 x 12cm/10 x 5in) lined with baking paper, and use a spatula to push and spread the mixture level and into the corners. Cover with baking paper and rest a heavy bag of rice or similar on top to weight it down. Let set in a cold environment for at least 24 hours. Slice into pieces and serve.

MELOCOTONES AL MOSCATEL

PEACHES POACHED IN SWEET MUSCAT WINE

In Spain, we love to remain at the table once we have finished eating. This is what we call *sobremesa*, **chatting and chatting before the siesta arrives. A sweet wine such as moscatel is the perfect ingredient to end a proper meal. This recipe includes fruit and this fantastic sweet wine combined. Try it!**

Serves 4

4 peaches, halved and stoned (nectarines or apricots work as well)

350–500ml (1½–2 cups) sweet muscat wine, such as Spanish moscatel

½ cinnamon stick

2 star anise

5 juniper berries

ice cream, clotted cream or natural yogurt, to serve, optional

Place the halved peaches in a deep pan; ideally they should fit snugly, holding each other. Add the moscatel, cinnamon, star anise and juniper berries and cook over a high heat until boiling, then immediately reduce the heat and simmer for 10 minutes, or until the peaches start to soften up. Don't overcook them; they should still be firm. Remove from the heat and leave to cool in the liquid, preferably overnight. This will help the flavours to develop within the fruit.

These peaches can be served with a wide range of accompaniments, such as ice cream, clotted cream or natural yogurt, for a more substantial dessert.

DESSERTS & SWEET TREATS

INDEX

A
acelgas con patatas 100
albóndigas a la trufa 48–9
alioli 27
  buñuelos de bacalao 14–15
  media luna de atún y alioli 29
alitas de pollo a la miel y limón 88–9
almejas a la marinera 70–1
almonds
  cazuela de langosta 140–1
  codornices con romesco 92–3
  turrón de almendra 180–1
almussafes 28
anchovies
  anchoas saladas con vinagre y pimentón 22–3
  arroz del senyoret 160–1
  banderillas 24–5
  cazuela de langosta 140–1
  vieiras gratinadas 78–9
apples: morcilla de burgos con manzana 52–3
apricots: melocotones al Moscatel 182–3
arroz
  arroz al horno 164–5
  arroz del senyoret 160–1
  arroz meloso de gambas y alcachofas 155
  arroz meloso de setas 158–9
artichokes: arroz meloso de gambas y alcachofas 155
asparagus
  espárragos con jamón 98–9
  huevos a la flamenca 82–3
  media luna de atún y alioli 29
atún con tomate 63
aubergines with honey 104–5
avocados: ensalada de aguacate y calabaza asada 116–17

B
bacalao con lentejas salteadas 138
bacalao y gambas al azafran con quinoa 62
bacon
  coca de requena 32–3
  cogollos de tudela con vinagreta de panceta 122–3
baked eggs with ham in tomato sauce 82–3
baked figs with tetilla cheese 171–3
baked rice with pork ribs and sausage 164–5
banderillas 24–5
beans
  fabes con almejas 148–9
  paella de marisco 152–4
  potaje canario 142–3
  potaje montañés 146–7
béchamel sauce: piquillos rellenos de setas 101
beef
  albóndigas a la trufa 48–9
  beef sandwich 28
  beef stew 139
  cachopo asturiano 45
  calabacín a la mallorquina 106–7
beer: berenjenas fritas con miel 104–5
berberechos al fino 69
berenjenas fritas con miel 104–5
black pudding
  coca de requena 32–3
  morcilla de burgos con manzana 52–3
  potaje montañés 146–7
black truffles: albóndigas a la trufa 48–9
bocadillos
  bocadillo de calamares 29
  bocadillos variados 28–9
brandy
  arroz del senyoret 160–1
  bacalao y gambas al azafran con quinoa 62
  cazuela de langosta 140–1
  estofado de corzo con setas 54–5
  fresas al brandy y crema de queso 170
  paella de marisco 152–4
  sangría de cava 12
bread
  bocadillo de calamares 29
  bocadillos variados 28–9
  calamares en su tinta 73
  carne gobernada 139
  chorizo al vino 44
  habas con chorizo 110–11
  huevos a la flamenca 82–3
  huevos con chorizo benedictinos 86–7
  media luna de atún y alioli 29
  morcilla de burgos con manzana 52–3
  pato con ciruelas 94–5
  piquillos rellenos de setas 101
  sopa de guisantes con jamón 134–5
  tosta de higos con jamón 20–1
breadcrumbs
  calabacín a la mallorquina 106–7
  cazuela de langosta 140–1
  vieiras gratinadas 78–9
broad beans with chorizo 110–11
buñuelos de bacalao 14–15
buñuelos de queso 16
butter beans
  fabes con almejas 148–9
  potaje montañés 146–7
butternut squash: ensalada de aguacate y calabaza asada 116–17

C
cabbage: potaje montañés 146–7
cachopo asturiano 45
calabacín a la mallorquina 106–7
calamares en su tinta 73
canapés 27
Canary Island meat and vegetable stew 142–3
capers
  carpaccio de atún 64–5
  coliflor con ajos vinagre y alcaparras 108–9
carne gobernada 139
carpaccio de atún 64–5
carrots
  coca de requena 32–3
  cordero al chilindrón 36–7
  ensaladilla rusa 121
  potaje canario 142–3
  ragú de carrilleras con pasta 144–5
cauliflower with garlic, vinegar and capers 108–9
cava 12
cazuela de langosta 140–1
champagne 12
champiñones gratinados 18–19
chard: acelgas con patatas 100
Cheddar cheese
  almussafes 28
  cachopo asturiano 45
cheese
  and alioli 27
  almussafes 28
  cachopo asturiano 45
  empanadillas de queso y spinaca 17
  ensalada de sandía, tomates y queso 124–5
  fruta secas al jerez con crema de manchego 175
  higos con tetilla asados 171–3
  macarrones con tomate y chorizo 40
  piquillos rellenos de setas 101
  tosta de higos con jamón 20–1
cheese cream: fresas al brandy y crema de queso 170
chestnuts: pato con ciruelas 94–5
chicken
  albóndigas a la trufa 48–9

alitas de pollo a la miel y
   limón 88–9
chuletitas de cordero
   marinadas 38–9
pinchos de pollo 91
pollastre al ast 90
chickpeas
   arroz al horno 164–5
   potaje canario 142–3
chicory: ensalada caliente
   de calamar, chorizo y
   endivias 126–7
chilled melon soup 136
chilled watermelon soup
   137
chilli peppers
   almejas a la marinera
      70–1
   bacalao con lentejas
      salteadas 138
   banderillas 24–5
   berberechos al fino 69
   carpaccio de atún 64–5
   cazuela de langosta
      140–1
   conejo en salmorejo 50–1
   revuelto de setas 84
chocolate ganache with
   olive oil and salt 174
chorizo
   chorizo, greens and bean
      stew 146–7
   chorizo al vino 44
   chorizo pâté and cheese
      sandwich 28
   coca de requena 32–3
   ensalada caliente de
      calamar, chorizo y
      endivias 126–7
   habas con chorizo
      110–11
   huevos a la flamenca
      82–3
   huevos con chorizo
      benedictinos 86–7
   macarrones con tomate y
      chorizo 40
   potaje montañés 146–7
   sepia con sobrasada o
      chorizo 76–7
chuletitas de cordero
   marinadas 38–9
ciabatta bread: pepito de
   ternera 28
clams
   almejas a la marinera
      70–1
   berberechos al fino 69
   clam and bean stew
      148–9

clotted cream: melocotones
   al Moscatel 182–3
coca de requena 32–3
cockles
   and alioli 27
   cockles in a dry sherry
      sauce 69
coconut cream: piña
   estofada con ron y
   crema de coco 168–9
cod
   arroz meloso de setas
      158–9
   bacalao y gambas al
      azafran con quinoa 62
   cod and lentil stew 138
   esgarraet valenciano
      128–9
   and prawns and quinoa
      with saffron sauce 62
   salt cod fritters 14–15
codornices con romesco
   92–3
cogollos de tudela con
   vinagreta de panceta
   122–3
Cointreau: sangría de cava
   12
coliflor con ajos vinagre y
   alcaparras 108–9
conejo en salmorejo 50–1
cordero al chilindrón 36–7
corn cobs: potaje canario
   142–3
cornichons see gherkins
courgettes
   calabacín a la mallorquina
      106–7
   pargo con calabacin
      espinaca y aceitunas
      60–1
   potaje canario 142–3
cream
   cremso de chocolate 174
   empanadillas de queso y
      spinaca 17
   ensaïmada mallorquina
      176–9
   fruta secas al jerez con
      crema de manchego
      175
   mejillones a la crema 72
   piña estofada con ron y
      crema de coco 168–9
cream cheese
   fruta secas al jerez con
      crema de manchego
      175
   tosta de higos con jamón
      20–1

creamy rice with prawns and
   artichokes 155
crème pâtissière:
   ensaïmada mallorquina
   176–9
cremso de chocolate 174
crisps: anchoas saladas
   con vinagre y pimentón
   22–3
currants: fruta secas al
   jerez con crema de
   manchego 175
cuttlefish
   grilled cuttlefish 74–5
   with sobrasada sausage or
      chorizo 76–7

D

dates: fruta secas al
   jerez con crema de
   manchego 175
deep-fried squid sandwich
   29
dried fruits stewed in sherry
   with a manchego
   cheese ganache 175
duck with prunes, chestnuts
   and pedro ximenez
   sherry 94–5

E

eggplant: berenjenas fritas
   con miel 104–5
eggs
   eggs benedict with
      spinach and chorizo
      hollandaise 86–7
   ensalada campera 119
   ensalada de canónigos,
      pimientos y atún 118
   ensaladilla rusa 121
   huevos a la flamenca
      82–3
   revuelto de setas 84
   tortilla Francesa 85
empanadillas de queso y
   spinaca 17
ensaïmada mallorquina
   176–9
ensalada
   ensalada caliente de
      calamar, chorizo y
      endivias 126–7
   ensalada campera 119
   ensalada de aguacate y
      calabaza asada 116–17
   ensalada de canónigos,
      pimientos y atún 118
   ensalada de cogollos,
      calamar y piquillos 120

ensalada de frisée y
   Granada 130–1
ensalada de sandía,
   tomates y queso
   124–5
ensaladilla rusa 121
esgarraet valenciano 128–9
espárragos con jamón 98–9
estofado de corzo con
   setas 54–5

F

fabes con almejas 148–9
figs: tosta de higos con
   jamón 20–1
fisherman-style clams
   70–1
focaccia: coca de requena
   32–3
French omelette 85
fresas al brandy y crema de
   queso 170
fried potatoes with spicy
   tomato sauce 26
frissée lettuce,
   pomegranate and olive
   salad 38, 130–1
fruta secas al jerez con
   crema de manchego
   175

G

Galician-style hake 58–9
garbanzo beans see
   chickpeas
garlic
   alioli 27
   arroz al horno 164–5
   arroz del senyoret 160–1
   arroz meloso de gambas y
      alcachofas 155
   arroz meloso de setas
      158–9
   bacalao con lentejas
      salteadas 138
   calabacín a la mallorquina
      106–7
   carne gobernada 139
   codornices con romesco
      92–3
   coliflor con ajos vinagre y
      alcaparras 108–9
   fabes con almejas 148–9
   habas con chorizo
      110–11
   paella de marisco 152–4
   pato con ciruelas 94–5
   potaje montañés 146–7
   ragú de carrilleras con
      pasta 144–5

gazpacho de sandía 137
gherkins
　banderillas 24–5
　ensaladilla rusa 121
goat cheese
　empanadillas de queso y spinaca 17
　ensalada de sandía, tomates y queso 124–5
green asparagus with Serrano ham 98–9
green beans
　paella de marisco 152–4
　potaje canario 142–3
greens
　potaje canario 142–3
　potaje montañés 146–7
grilled cuttlefish 74–5
grilled lettuce with a sweet and sour bacon vinaigrette 122–3

H
habas con chorizo 110–11
hake
　Galician-style hake 58–9
　hake a la romana with mayonnaise 66–7
ham
　berberechos al fino 69
　cachopo asturiano 45
　champiñones gratinados 18–19
　espárragos con jamón 98–9
　huevos a la flamenca 82–3
　potaje montañés 146–7
　sopa de guisantes con jamón 134–5
　sopa de melón 136
　tosta de higos con jamón 20–1
hazelnuts: codornices con romesco 92–3
higos con tetilla asados 171–3
honey
　almussafes 28
　berenjenas fritas con miel 104–5
　chuletitas de cordero marinadas 38–9
　cogollos de tudela con vinagreta de panceta 122–3
　honey and lemon chicken wings 88–9

morcilla de burgos con manzana 52–3
pinchos de pollo 91
turrón de almendra 180–1
hot pan-fried squid, lettuce and piquillo pepper salad 120
huevos
　huevos a la flamenca 82–3
　huevos con chorizo benedictinos 86–7

I
ice cream: melocotones al Moscatel 182–3

J
juniper berries: melocotones al Moscatel 182–3

L
lager: berenjenas fritas con miel 104–5
lamb
　chuletitas de cordero marinadas 38–9
　slow-cooked lamb and pepper stew 36–7
lamb's lettuce, roasted red pepper and tuna salad 118
langoustines: paella de marisco 152–4
leeks
　arroz del senyoret 160–1
　bacalao y gambas al azafran con quinoa 62
　carne gobernada 139
　paella de marisco 152–4
lemons
　alitas de pollo a la miel y limón 88–9
　codornices con romesco 92–3
　pinchos de pollo 91
lentils: bacalao con lentejas salteadas 138
lettuce
　cogollos de tudela con vinagreta de panceta 122–3
　ensalada de aguacate y calabaza asada 116–17
　ensalada de canónigos, pimientos y atún 118
　ensalada de cogollos, calamar y piquillos 120

ensalada de frisée y Granada 130–1
Frisée lettuce, pomegranate and olive salad 38
media luna de atún y alioli 29
lima beans see butter beans
lobster and saffron pasta stew 140–1
lord's paella, with shellfish but no shells 160–1

M
macarrones con tomate y chorizo 40
espárragos con jamón 98–9
fruta secas al jerez con crema de manchego 175
mango: carpaccio de atún 64–5
marinated chicken skewers 91
marrow: potaje canario 142–3
mayonnaise
　alioli 27
　bocadillo de calamares 29
　champiñones gratinados 18–19
　ensaladilla rusa 121
　media luna de atún y alioli 29
　merluza a la romana 66–7
meatballs in black truffle sauce 48–9
meat focaccia 32–3
media luna de atún y alioli 29
mejillones
　mejillones a la crema 72
　mejillones en vinagrete 68
melocotones al Moscatel 182–3
melon
　ensalada de sandía, tomates y queso 124–5
　gazpacho de sandía 137
　sopa de melón 136
　tosta de higos con jamón 20–1
merluza
merluza a la gallega 58–9
merluza a la romana 66–7

mint leaves: sangría de cava 12
mojo dulce sauce: torreznos con mojo dulce 41
Moorish marinated lamb cutlets 38–9
morcilla
　arroz al horno 164–5
　morcilla de burgos con manzana 52–3
mushrooms
　arroz meloso de setas 158–9
　estofado de corzo con setas 54–5
　mushroom gratin with ham mayonnaise 18–19
　piquillos rellenos de setas 101
　revuelto de setas 84
mussels
　and alioli 27
　berberechos al fino 69
　mussels in a cream sauce 72
　mussels in a vegetable and tomato vinaigrette 68

N
nectarines: melocotones al Moscatel 182–3
new potato, tuna and egg salad 119
nuts
　codornices con romesco 92–3
　ensalada de aguacate y calabaza asada 116–17
　fruta secas al jerez con crema de manchego 175
　morcilla de burgos con manzana 52–3
　tosta de higos con jamón 20–1
　turrón de almendra 180–1

O
olives
banderillas 24–5
　carpaccio de atún 64–5
　ensalada campera 119
　ensalada de canónigos, pimientos y atún 118
　ensalada de cogollos, calamar y piquillos 120

ensalada de frisée y Granada 130–1
ensaladilla rusa 121
Frisée lettuce, pomegranate and olive salad 38, 130–1
pargo con calabacin espinaca y aceitunas 60–1
omelette, French 85
onions
    banderillas 24–5
    estofado de corzo con setas 54–5
oranges: sangría de cava 12

P

paellas
    arroz del senyoret 160–1
    arroz meloso de setas 158–9
    paella de marisco 152–4
pancetta
    coca de requena 32–3
    cogollos de tudela con vinagreta de panceta 122–3
pan-fried figs, serrano ham, cream cheese and walnuts on toast 20–1
pan-fried squid with spicy chorizo and chicory salad 126–7
paprika see pimentón
pargo con calabacin espinaca y aceitunas 60–1
Parmesan cheese: macarrones con tomate y chorizo 40
pasta
    cazuela de langosta 140–1
    macarrones con tomate y chorizo 40
    ragú de carrilleras con pasta 144–5
pastry
ensaïmada mallorquina 176–9
pastry parcels filled with spinach, raisins and goat cheese 17
patatas
    patatas bravas 26
    patatas machaconas 112–13
pâté: albóndigas a la trufa 48–9

pato con ciruelas 94–5
peaches poached in Muscatel wine 182–3
pears: sangría de cava 12
peas
    ensaladilla rusa 121
    pargo con calabacin espinaca y aceitunas 60–1
    pea soup with Serrano ham 134–5
penne pasta with chorizo and tomato sauce 40
pepito de ternera 28
peppers
    almejas a la marinera 70–1
    arroz meloso de setas 158–9
    atún con tomate 63
    bacalao con lentejas salteadas 138
    banderillas 24–5
    berberechos al fino 69
    carne gobernada 139
    carpaccio de atún 64–5
    cazuela de langosta 140–1
    coca de requena 32–3
    codornices con romesco 92–3
    conejo en salmorejo 50–1
    ensalada campera 119
    ensalada de canónigos, pimientos y atún 118
    ensalada de cogollos, calamar y piquillos 120
    esgarraet valenciano 128–9
    gazpacho de sandía 137
    huevos a la flamenca 82–3
    media luna de atún y alioli 29
    mejillones en vinagreta 68
    paella de marisco 152–4
    piquillos rellenos de setas 101
pickled cucumbers see gherkins
pickled onions: banderillas 24–5
pig cheeks: ragú de carrilleras con pasta 144–5
pimentón
    acelgas con patatas 100
    alitas de pollo a la miel y limón 88–9

almejas a la marinera 70–1
anchoas saladas con vinagre y pimentón 22–3
arroz al horno 164–5
arroz del senyoret 160–1
arroz meloso de gambas y alcachofas 155
arroz meloso de setas 158–9
atún con tomate 63
bacalao con lentejas salteadas 138
bacalao y gambas al azafran con quinoa 62
carne gobernada 139
chuletitas de cordero marinadas 38–9
coca de requena 32–3
codornices con romesco 92–3
cogollos de tudela con vinagreta de panceta 122–3
conejo en salmorejo 50–1
estofado de corzo con setas 54–5
huevos a la flamenca 82–3
huevos con chorizo benedictinos 86–7
paella de marisco 152–4
pargo con calabacin espinaca y aceitunas 60–1
patatas machaconas 112–13
pinchos de pollo 91
potaje canario 142–3
potaje montañés 146–7
sopa de guisantes con jamón 134–5
sopa de melón 136
pimientos choriceros: codornices con romesco 92–3
piña estofada con ron y crema de coco 168–9
pinchos de pollo 91
pineapple: piña estofada con ron y crema de coco 168–9
pine nuts: morcilla de burgos con manzana 52–3
piquillo peppers
    ensalada de cogollos, calamar y piquillos 120

media luna de atún y alioli 29
piquillo peppers stuffed with mushrooms (piquillos rellenos de setas) 101
pistachios: fruta secas al jerez con crema de manchego 175
poached caramelized pineapple in rum with coconut cream 168–9
pollastre al ast 90
pomegranate
    ensalada de frisée y Granada 130–1
    Frisée lettuce, pomegranate and olive salad 38, 130–1
pork
    albóndigas a la trufa 48–9
    arroz al horno 164–5
    calabacín a la mallorquina 106–7
    chuletitas de cordero marinadas 38–9
    patatas machaconas 112–13
    potaje canario 142–3
    potaje montañés 146–7
    ragú de carrilleras con pasta 144–5
    torreznos con mojo dulce 41
potaje
    potaje canario 142–3
    potaje montañés 146–7
potatoes
    acelgas con patatas 100
    arroz al horno 164–5
    buñuelos de bacalao 14–15
    carne gobernada 139
    coca de requena 32–3
    ensalada campera 119
    ensaladilla rusa 121
    estofado de corzo con setas 54–5
    merluza a la gallega 58–9
    patatas bravas 26
    patatas machaconas 112–13
    pato con ciruelas 94–5
    potaje canario 142–3
    torreznos con mojo dulce 41
prawns
    arroz del senyoret 160–1

arroz meloso de gambas y alcachofas 155
bacalao y gambas al azafran con quinoa 62
paella de marisco 152–4
prunes
  fruta secas al jerez con crema de manchego 175
  pato con ciruelas 94–5
pumpkin seeds: ensalada de frisée y Granada 130–1

Q
quails: codornices con romesco 92–3
quinoa: bacalao y gambas al azafran con quinoa 62

R
rabbit with a canary islands sauce 50–1
ragú de carrilleras con pasta 144–5
raisins: empanadillas de queso y spinaca 17
red onions
  cogollos de tudela con vinagreta de panceta 122–3
  ensalada campera 119
red peppers
  arroz meloso de setas 158–9
  bacalao con lentejas salteadas 138
  carne gobernada 139
  cazuela de langosta 140–1
  codornices con romesco 92–3
  cordero al chilindrón 36–7
  empanadillas de queso y spinaca 17
  ensalada campera 119
  ensalada de canónigos, pimientos y atún 118
  esgarraet valenciano 128–9
  gazpacho de sandía 137
  paella de marisco 152–4
red snapper with courgette, olives and spinach 60–1
revuelto de setas 84
rice
  arroz al horno 164–5
  arroz del senyoret 160–1
  arroz meloso de gambas y alcachofas 155

arroz meloso de setas 158–9
paella de marisco 152–4
roasted almond nougat 180–1
roasted red pepper and salt cod salad 128–9
rolled flaky pastry 176–9
romesco sauce
  buñuelos de bacalao 14–15
  codornices con romesco 92–3
rum: piña estofada con ron y crema de coco 168–9
runner beans
  paella de marisco 152–4
  potaje canario 142–3
Russian potato salad 121

S
saffron
  arroz al horno 164–5
  arroz del senyoret 160–1
  arroz meloso de gambas y alcachofas 155
  arroz meloso de setas 158–9
  bacalao y gambas al azafran con quinoa 62
  cazuela de langosta 140–1
  fabes con almejas 148–9
  paella de marisco 152–4
salads
  cogollos de tudela con vinagreta de panceta 122–3
  ensalada caliente de calamar, chorizo y endivias 126–7
  ensalada campera 119
  ensalada de cogollos, calamar y piquillos 120
  ensalada de frisée y Granada 130–1
  ensalada de sandía, tomates y queso 124–5
  ensaladilla rusa 121
  esgarraet valenciano 128–9
  Frisée lettuce, pomegranate and olive salad 38, 130–1
  lamb's lettuce, roasted red pepper and tuna salad 118

salad of avocado, lettuce, butternut squash and walnuts 116–17
salmorejo sauce: conejo en salmorejo 50–1
salt cod
  arroz meloso de setas 158–9
  esgarraet valenciano 128–9
  salt cod fritters 14–15
salted anchovies
  banderillas 24–5
  salted anchovies with paprika and vinegar 22–3
sandwiches, assorted 28–9
sangría de cava 12
sardines: anchoas saladas con vinagre y pimentón 22–3
sauces
  alioli 27
  béchamel 101
  Mojo Dulce 41
  romesco 14–15, 92–3
sausages
  arroz al horno 164–5
  coca de requena 32–3
  see also chorizo
scallions see spring onions
scallop and serrano ham gratin served in a shell 78–9
scrambled eggs with wild mushrooms 84
seafood paella 152–4
sepia
  sepia a la plancha con ajilimoji 74–5
  sepia con sobrasada o chorizo 76–7
Serrano ham
  berberechos al fino 69
  cachopo asturiano 45
  espárragos con jamón 98–9
  huevos a la flamenca 82–3
  potaje montañés 146–7
  sopa de guisantes con jamón 134–5
  tosta de higos con jamón 20–1
  vieiras gratinadas 78–9
sherry
  bacalao con lentejas salteadas 138
  berberechos al fino 69

espárragos con jamón 98–9
fruta secas al jerez con crema de manchego 175
higos con tetilla asados 171–3
pato con ciruelas 94–5
skewered pickles 24–5
slow-cooked pork belly with a sweet, spicy and sour sauce 41
smoked pimentón
  patatas machaconas 112–13
  potaje canario 142–3
Sobrasada de Mallorca sausages
  almussafes 28
  ensaïmada mallorquina 176–9
  sepia con sobrasada o chorizo 76–7
sopa
  sopa de guisantes con Jamón 134–5
  sopa de melón 136
soups
  chilled melon soup 136
  gazpacho de sandía 137
  pea soup with Serrano ham 134–5
soupy rice with mushrooms and cod 158–9
sourdough bread: carne gobernada 139
Spanish cordon bleu 45
Spanish rice black pudding with caramelized apple 52–3
Spanish style roast chicken 90
spatchcock quail with a roasted nut sauce 92–3
spiced mashed potatoes with crispy pork belly 112–13
spinach
  empanadillas de queso y spinaca 17
  huevos con chorizo benedictinos 86–7
  pargo con calabacin espinaca y aceitunas 60–1
spring greens
  potaje canario 142–3
  potaje montañés 146–7
spring onions

albóndigas a la trufa 48–9
ensalada caliente de calamar, chorizo y endivias 126–7
fabes con almejas 148–9
mejillones a la crema 72
mejillones en vinagreta 68
squash: potaje canario 142–3
squid
    arroz del senyoret 160–1
    arroz meloso de gambas y alcachofas 155
    bocadillo de calamares 29
    ensalada caliente de calamar, chorizo y endivias 126–7
    ensalada de cogollos, calamar y piquillos 120
    paella de marisco 152–4
    squid in black ink sauce 73
steaks: cachopo asturiano 45
stews
    bacalao con lentejas salteadas 138
    carne gobernada 139
    cazuela de langosta 140–1
    potaje canario 142–3
    potaje montañés 146–7
    stewed pig cheeks with pasta 144–5
strawberries
    sangría de cava 12
    strawberries poached in brandy with a cream cheese 170
stuffed courgettes 106–7
sweet pimentón
    acelgas con patatas 100
    alitas de pollo a la miel y limón 88–9
    almejas a la marinera 70–1
    arroz al horno 164–5
    arroz del senyoret 160–1
    arroz meloso de gambas y alcachofas 155
    arroz meloso de setas 158–9
    atún con tomate 63
    bacalao con lentejas salteadas 138
    bacalao y gambas al azafran con quinoa 62
    carne gobernada 139
    chuletitas de cordero marinadas 38–9

coca de requena 32–3
codornices con romesco 92–3
cogollos de tudela con vinagreta de panceta 122–3
conejo en salmorejo 50–1
estofado de corzo con setas 54–5
huevos a la flamenca 82–3
huevos con chorizo benedictinos 86–7
paella de marisco 152–4
pargo con calabacin espinaca y aceitunas 60–1
patatas machaconas 112–13
pinchos de pollo 91
potaje montañés 146–7
sopa de guisantes con jamón 134–5
sopa de melón 136
Swiss chard with potatoes 100

T
Tetilla cheese: higos con tetilla asados 171–3
tomatoes
    arroz al horno 164–5
    arroz del senyoret 160–1
    arroz meloso de gambas y alcachofas 155
    arroz meloso de setas 158–9
    atún con tomate 63
    calamares en su tinta 73
    coca de requena 32–3
    codornices con romesco 92–3
    ensalada caliente de calamar, chorizo y endivias 126–7
    ensalada campera 119
    ensalada de sandía, tomates y queso 124–5
    estofado de corzo con setas 54–5
    gazpacho de sandía 137
    huevos a la flamenca 82–3
    macarrones con tomate y chorizo 40
    mejillones en vinagreta 68
    paella de marisco 152–4

patatas bravas 26
ragú de carrilleras con pasta 144–5
sepia con sobrasada o chorizo 76–7
torreznos con mojo dulce 41
tortilla Francesa 85
tosta de higos con jamón 20–1
truffles: albóndigas a la trufa 48–9
tuna
    ensalada campera 119
    ensalada de canónigos, pimientos y atún 118
    ensaladilla rusa 121
    tuna and alioli sandwich with piquillo peppers 29
    tuna carpaccio with olive, mango and caper dressing 64–5
    tuna in tomato sauce 63
turkey: albóndigas a la trufa 48–9
turrón de almendra 180–1

V
venison and wild mushroom stew with olive mash (my family style) 54–5
vieiras gratinadas 78–9
vinaigrettes
    cogollos de tudela con vinagreta de panceta 122–3
    ensalada de aguacate y calabaza asada 116–17
    ensalada de sandía, tomates y queso 124–5
vinegar: anchoas saladas con vinagre y pimentón 22–3

W
walnuts
    ensalada de aguacate y calabaza asada 116–17
    tosta de higos con jamón 20–1
watermelon
    gazpacho de sandía 137
    watermelon, tomato, coriander and goat's cheese salad 124–5
white anchovies: banderillas 24–5

white asparagus: espárragos con jamón 98–9
wine
    almejas a la marinera 70–1
    arroz del senyoret 160–1
    bacalao y gambas al azafran con quinoa 62
    calamares en su tinta 73
    carne gobernada 139
    cazuela de langosta 140–1
    chorizo al vino 44
    conejo en salmorejo 50–1
    estofado de corzo con setas 54–5
    mejillones en vinagreta 68
    paella de marisco 152–4
    piquillos rellenos de setas 101
    ragú de carrilleras con pasta 144–5
    sepia con sobrasada o chorizo 76–7

Y
yogurt: melocotones al Moscatel 182–3

Z
zucchini see courgettes

ACKNOWLEDGEMENTS

I write this with a big smile on my face and tears in my eyes because I am so thankful and feel so fortunate to have in my life the people that I do.

The last couple of years have been a rollercoaster but I am so happy with how things have worked out. Thanks to all of you the future looks brighter than ever.

Familia, gracias por todo vuestro apoyo y amor incondicional. Aunque estemos muy unidos se os echa mucho de menos desde la distancia. Especial mención para mi padre y hermano que me habéis dado siempre todo lo mejor y habéis velado por mi, lo tengo presente en cada minuto de mi vida. Os quiero.

Gracias madre por todo, especialmente por cuidadarnos con esa manera tan especial que siempre has tenido de hacerlo y por darnos tanto amor. Nuestros corazones estarán llenos para siempre.

Dani, gracias por tu ayuda y amistad, indudablemente todo es más llevadero a la par! Jaja

I am especially thankful to my wife Sandra for being the best partner one could wish for, for loving me for who I am and for supporting me all the way, which is no mean feat, haha! And to my kids Noah, Oscar and Eduard for bringing the greatest joy to our world. Watching you grow is our daily inspiration.

Sarah and Sofie, hooray, we did it again! Thank you for believing in me from the start and helping me to get this book off the ground. I am so glad you are as crazy as I am for giving me a second chance – what a relief! It's such a pleasure to work with you and your professionalism is appreciated.

Martin, Martin, Martin… like a good Rioja, you just get better with time, don't you? I seriously thought the first book was unbeatable in terms of photography but you did it again, mate. I am so impressed. Thank you so much for making my food shine and for the fun.

Rosie, Sian and Polly, thank you for making the recipes look as they meant to, which wasn't an easy task at all. We aimed high and I feel we achieved it – cracking job.

And one last big thank you to everyone who has bought any of my books in the past or supported my work somehow, I genuinely appreciate it and I hope they have come handy at some point!

ABOUT THE AUTHOR

Madrid-born Omar Allibhoy, also known as 'The Spanish Chef', began his career training under legendary chef Ferran Adrià, then with Gordon Ramsay in London, who dubbed him the 'Antonio Banderas of cooking'. Since opening his first restaurant in 2010, he has been on a mission to showcase just how simple cooking Spanish cuisine at home can be. Omar is committed to being at the forefront of representing the wonderful food of Spain in the UK and has picked up multiple awards along the way. Omar has maintained a career as a successful TV chef and is the author of *Tapas Revolution* and *Paella*. As well as running a highly regarded catering company, he runs an online deli where you can get Spanish ingredients delivered to your doorstep anywhere in mainland UK. More info on his website www.thespanishchef.com.

Quadrille, Penguin Random House UK, One Embassy Gardens, 8 Viaduct Gardens, London SW11 7BW

Quadrille Publishing Limited is part of the Penguin Random House group of companies whose addresses can be found at global.penguinrandomhouse.com

Penguin Random House UK

Copyright © Omar Allibhoy 2025
Photography © Martin Poole 2016
Design © Quadrille 2025

Omar Allibhoy has asserted his right to be identified as the author(s) of this Work in accordance with the Copyright, Designs and Patents Act 1988

Penguin Random House values and supports copyright. Copyright fuels creativity, encourages diverse voices, promotes freedom of expression and supports a vibrant culture. Thank you for purchasing an authorized edition of this book and for respecting intellectual property laws by not reproducing, scanning or distributing any part of it by any means without permission. You are supporting authors and enabling Penguin Random House to continue to publish books for everyone. No part of this book may be used or reproduced in any manner for the purpose of training artificial intelligence technologies or systems. In accordance with Article 4(3) of the DSM Directive 2019/790, Penguin Random House expressly reserves this work from the text and data mining exception.

Published by Quadrille in 2025

www.penguin.co.uk

A CIP catalogue record for this book is available from the British Library

ISBN 978 1 83783 348 1

10 9 8 7 6 5 4 3 2 1

Managing Director Sarah Lavelle

Project Editors Céline Hughes and Sofie Shearman

Designer Alicia House

Cover Illustration Jordan Amy Lee

Photographer Martin Poole

Food Stylist Rosie Reynolds

Food Stylist Assistant Sian Henley

Prop Stylist Polly Webb Wilson

Head of Production Stephen Lang

Production Controller Sumayyah Waheed

Colour reproduction by F1

Printed and bound in China by C&C Offset Printing Co., Ltd.

The authorised representative in the EEA is Penguin Random House Ireland, Morrison Chambers, 32 Nassau Street, Dublin D02 YH68.

Penguin Random House is committed to a sustainable future for our business, our readers and our planet. This book is made from Forest Stewardship Council® certified paper.

FSC MIX Paper | Supporting responsible forestry
www.fsc.org FSC® C018179